THE LANGUAGE OF SEXUAL MISCONDUCT CASES

THE LANGUAGE OF SEXUAL MISCONDUCT CASES

Roger W. Shuy

OXFORD
UNIVERSITY PRESS

OXFORD
UNIVERSITY PRESS

Oxford University Press is a department of the University of Oxford.
It furthers the University's objective of excellence in research, scholarship,
and education by publishing worldwide.

Oxford New York
Auckland Cape Town Dar es Salaam Hong Kong Karachi
Kuala Lumpur Madrid Melbourne Mexico City Nairobi
New Delhi Shanghai Taipei Toronto

With offices in
Argentina Austria Brazil Chile Czech Republic France Greece
Guatemala Hungary Italy Japan Poland Portugal Singapore
South Korea Switzerland Thailand Turkey Ukraine Vietnam

Published in the United States of America by
Oxford University Press
198 Madison Avenue, New York, NY 10016

Library of Congress Cataloging-in-Publication Data
Shuy, Roger W.
The language of sexual misconduct cases / Roger W. Shuy.
p. cm.
Includes bibliographical references and index.
ISBN 978-0-19-992696-1 (hardcover : alk. paper) 1. Sex crimes—United States—Cases. 2. Sexual harassment—Law and legislation—United States—Cases. 3. Child sexual abuse—United States—Cases. 4. Sex and law—United States—Interpretation and construction. 5. Law—United States—Language. I. Title.
KF9325.A52S58 2012
345.73'02530264—dc23
2011050346

ISBN 978-0-19-992696-1

1 3 5 7 9 8 6 4 2
Printed in the United States of America
on acid-free paper

I wish to give special thanks to my daughter, Katie Shuy, for her editing and proofreading assistance in the writing of this book. Her professional skills in writing and editing were, as usual, extremely helpful. I also want to thank Professor Larry Solan of the Brooklyn Law School and Professors Jeff Renz and Fritz Snyder of the University of Montana Law School for helping me try to understand some of the legal aspects of sexual misconduct laws. I can only hope that I was an apt learner. In addition, my thanks go to Professor Robert Leonard of Hofstra University, who was my partner in analyzing some of the cases described in this book.

CONTENTS

SECTION TWO
SEXUAL MISCONDUCT OF AN ADULT WITH A CHILD

SECTION THREE
SEXUAL MISCONDUCT OF AN ADULT WITH ANOTHER ADULT

SECTION FOUR
PROSECUTION AND DEFENSE TOOLS

THE LANGUAGE OF SEXUAL MISCONDUCT CASES

[1]

INTRODUCTION

Few crimes are more disturbing than sexual misconduct, and most people find such cases even more disturbing when it is a child that has been molested. Therefore it is with considerable caution and discomfort that I write this book. I'm usually disquieted when a defense lawyer calls me for assistance in such cases, for I know that the evidence will be especially unpleasant and wrenching. It's usually the defense lawyer who calls me, because prosecutors, who have never asked for my help in sexual misconduct cases, seem to be confident that their intelligence gathering and analysis will lead to a certain conviction. It makes no difference which side asks for my help, however, because analysis of the language evidence would be exactly the same no matter who asks for it. Since more and more charges of sexual misconduct are being brought to trial, this area of potential linguistic analysis seems to be an important one to address.

Of course, this book is not the first to deal with sexual misconduct, at least as the term is broadly understood. Much has been written about language in the context of child sexual abuse as well as the police interviewing and courtroom language that is used as sexual abuse cases are tried. For example, Janet Cotterill's collection, *The Language of Sexual Crime* (2007), is an important resource for those who are interested in the way language is used in rape trials. For example, Susan Berk-Seligson's chapter in that book, describing a case in which a man is charged with both murder and rape, contains important analyses of the language of both the interviewer and the suspect in the police interviews, although her conclusions do not agree with the findings of the eleven cases I present here.

Gregory Matoesian has also provided excellent analyses of rape case trials in his books, *Reproducing Rape: Domination through Talk in the Courtroom* (1993) and *Law and the Language of Identity: Discourse in the William Kennedy Smith Rape Trial* (2001). Susan Ehrlich deals with the important concept of consensual sex in her book, *Representing Rape: Language and Sexual Consent* (2001). Robin Lakoff's book, *The Language War* (2000) and Norma Mendoza-Denton's article, "Pregnant Pauses: Silence and Authority in the Anita Hill–Clarence Thomas Hearings" (1995), shed considerable light not only on the linguistically relevant language aspects of Justice Clarence Thomas's confirmation hearings, but also on the growth of concerns about sexual harassment in the United States.

While previous books and articles by linguists have focused primarily on the language used by attorneys and judges in rape trials or sexual harassment issues, certain aspects of sexual misconduct have not attracted the amount of linguistic attention that they might. Somewhat different from this previous work, I turn my attention to certain aspects of sexual misconduct that I believe have hitherto not received the linguistic attention they deserve: the language evidence of sexual misconduct that takes place in the workplace, cases of adult-on-child sexual misconduct within a family that are recalled at a later time, and adult–adult sexual misconduct cases involving improper touching and fondling (but not intercourse), also including solicitation of sex.

Throughout the case descriptions in this book I examine the approaches used by the police as they attempt to gather intelligence, noting in particular where these approaches are not used effectively. I also assess their competence in producing electronic recordings to be used as evidence, their language as they interview suspects and witnesses, their management and execution of confrontation calls and meetings made by complainants to suspects, their use of one-way communication evidence, and the degree to which they consider both the suspect's and complainant's agendas and intentions as these are revealed both by the context in which the events occurred and by the schemas revealed by the suspects, complainants, and police.

Also described throughout the eleven cases presented in this book are the linguistic analytical tools that are available but often unused by both the prosecution and the defense. I argue that there is a productive sequence in which these tools should be used, beginning with the larger language units: identifying the speech event in which the communication takes place, the schemas of the participants, the agendas of the speakers as revealed by the topics they introduce as well as their responses to the topics of others, and the speech acts used by all participants. After the analysis deals with these larger language units, it can be productive to examine the smaller language units, including the use or nonuse of the cooperative principle, the conversational strategies employed by the participants, the use or nonuse of the recency principle, the occasions in which ambiguity occurs and how it is dealt with, and finally, the smallest language units of all, the grammatical and lexical features. Throughout the book I argue that it is common for lawyers to focus on the smaller alleged "smoking gun" features while overlooking how these smaller language units can be explained by the overall language context in which they appear.

Linguists who work with various types of law cases try to provide salience to the most important linguistic features relevant to a given case, but not every case requires all of the analytical tools available in the linguist's toolbox. Focusing only on the linguistic procedures appropriate to a given case prevents lawyers from becoming bogged down with more information than they need for their immediate case needs. In the same way, the linguistic consultants need to avoid being mired in all of the legal issues relating to an individual case, which, though they may be essential to the lawyers, are often less salient for the linguist's immediate task of helping them and their clients. The retaining lawyers can educate their consulting linguists about the immediate legal matters relating to their specific cases and it is up to the linguist to choose which linguistic tools relate to those legal matters.

It is never easy to write for two audiences at the same time, for trying to do so opens the door to criticism by lawyers, who may feel that the book does not describe the legal issues comprehensively, and by linguists, who may not feel that it deals with linguistic theories and principles to the fullest extent possible. Both criticisms are undoubtedly justifiable because this is what happens when writers try to reach two different audiences simultaneously.

Therefore this book is neither a treatise on law nor a comprehensive introduction to linguistics. It is, instead, an effort to help bridge the gap between two fields that might otherwise not know each other well enough. Most linguists are not lawyers, and most lawyers are not linguists, yet for their combined efforts to work efficiently there has to be a common meeting ground about the way linguistic analysis applies to individual situations. It is rare for lawyers and linguists to be experts in both fields at the same time, but since my goal is to serve as a mediator between different fields, I want to present just enough information about both fields to provide mutual comprehension on focused topics. At any rate, there is more than a little overlap between linguistics and law, since law is largely about the way language is written in statutes and other authoritative documents, spoken in legal settings, and used as evidence. The focus here is on the latter category—how language is used as evidence.

Following my usual procedure, this book briefly outlines laws relating to various aspects and categories of adult sexual misconduct and then shows how linguistic analysis was used in eleven fairly representative cases. It is my hope that linguists will be aided by the analyses provided here and that lawyers who read this book will gain insights about how they can use linguists in their sexual misconduct cases. When feasible, I have also included much of the language evidence in these cases so that students and others can analyze it themselves.

Readers of my previous books will notice that I commonly include the names of the participants along with case citations. Because of the sensitive nature of sexual misconduct cases, I have decided to preserve the anonymity of the participants in this book, and have thus removed their names and other potentially identifying features. The only exception is the case of a U.S. senator that was virtually impossible to treat anonymously. All of these cases, however, are real.

I make no claim that most people charged with crimes, including sexual misconduct, are innocent, for that would be wrong. Some suspects and defendants are clearly guilty and some are innocent. Still other suspects are guilty of some of the charges made against them but are not guilty all of all of the charges. In some cases that are not discussed here, after analyzing the evidence I made it clear to the retaining attorneys that there was little or nothing that linguistic analysis could do that would help their clients. When this happened, my work ended and the lawyers could either try to convince their clients to accept whatever plea they could get or to take their chances and go to trial anyway. All of the cases discussed in this book contained some uncertainty in how the evidence might be construed, otherwise they would not be worth discussing.

The sexual misconduct cases used in this book are divided into three sections. The first section describes the use of linguistic analysis in sexual misconduct that occurred in a workplace setting. Offices, businesses, and schools are the usual settings for such accusations, where bosses, medical workers, and teachers are the source of many such complaints. As chapter 2 points out, like sexual harassment, sexual misconduct usually occurs when a person in authority engages in an uninvited sexual activity with a subordinate. Whereas sexual harassment is defined as behaviors that are found to be threatening or disturbing, sexual misconduct, as treated in this book, refers to real or alleged wrongful, uninvited, and improper physical sexual conduct, but not rape.

Section I describes two cases relating to the alleged sexual misconduct of doctors with their patients. One case took place in the office of a sheriff, and the sexual misconduct of a U.S. senator caused him to be charged with improperly touching a number of women in his office. He also was investigated simultaneously for other criminal acts.

Section II reports sexual misconduct cases in which adult family members are alleged to have engaged in improper physical sexual acts with young children. Although the accuser's memory is usually an important issue in such cases, analysis of false memory goes beyond linguistics proper and will not be treated here. One case stems from a child's dream that is reported by her mother. The second case involves an earlier alleged sexual act recalled by a teenage minor who woke up in an inebriated condition and claimed that her stepfather was sexually assaulting her. The third case describes a teenage girl's memories of her stepfather's sexual abuse that allegedly took place some five or six years earlier. A fourth case is about the alleged sexual intentions of a man who, in the middle of the night, claimed to have confusedly crawled into the wrong bed where his stepdaughter was sleeping and subsequently felt her breast.

Section III concerns sexual misconduct allegations of adults with other adults. One case describes college students whose evening dinner date went terribly wrong. The second case involves a salesman who was accused of intentionally engaging in uninvited sexual acts with a lonely hairdresser while he was installing equipment at her shop. The third case describes a police sting that caught a famous athlete who was allegedly soliciting sex from a female police decoy on a city street.

In the second to final chapter I describe the techniques and processes used by law enforcement and prosecutors in these cases, showing the problems they had in carrying out their work. In the final chapter I reprise the linguistic tools used in each of these cases with more theoretical detail than is found in the case analysis chapters.

In my opinion, the most important aspects of this book are the conclusions I have come to after more than three decades of working on cases involving conversational and interview evidence. I first reported these in my book, *The Language of Perjury Cases* (2011), but I go into more detail in the current book. As noted above, my thesis is that lawyers are too enamored with finding "smoking gun" evidence in isolated words and phrases that the evidence provides. I argue that the process of intelligence analysis used by prosecutors, defense lawyers, and linguistic consultants would do well to begin with the larger language units before examining the smaller ones, such as isolated words and phrases.

Some readers may be disappointed that I do not include all of the outcomes of the law cases in which linguistic consultation played a role. I do not reveal them because trial results are the sole responsibility of lawyers and juries, not expert witnesses. In some of the cases that I report here, I actually never learned the jury's decision, but even when I did hear the verdicts, it made no particular difference to me in my role as a consulting linguist. My goal here, and in all the other cases I've worked on over the past three decades, is to present the analyses used in those cases, which was often helpful and sometimes less so. I expect that readers will come to their own conclusions about how useful they were.

Readers may also notice that in all eleven of the cases described here the retaining lawyers represented the accused party. One reason for this imbalance is that in the United States it is rare when a prosecutor calls on a forensic linguist to testify or even to consult. I can only speculate about why this is the case, but it would seem that prosecutors may believe that they have all of the evidence they need without requiring any linguistics experts to assist them. As I've said in other books and articles, the analysis of any competent forensic linguist would be the same, no matter who the retaining lawyer might be. Experts analyze the existing language evidence for what it is.

Readers are also warned that because of the nature of the cases, the language in this book is sometimes sexually explicit, especially the language evidence used at trial.

Most of the cases in this book include undercover tape recordings that were used as evidence by the prosecution. I consulted with the attorneys in all of these cases and was paid for my analyses.

[2]

A BRIEF OVERVIEW OF SEXUAL MISCONDUCT LAW AND PROSECUTION

The term "sexual misconduct" includes a variety of behaviors that people use in order to get sexual gratification from another person. The term includes a range of behaviors, including rape, sexual harassment, and sexual assault, along with other conduct that is carried out without the victim's consent. Threatening or intimidating the victim is included in this law. Sexual misconduct usually involves touching, kissing, or fondling other persons without their consent; exposing the genitals in an unwanted manner; having sexual intercourse with another person in front of other people; public nudity; exposing someone to child pornography; child molestation, including making sexually suggestive statements to a child; having deviate sexual intercourse in a public place or before other people; forcing another person to touch someone's genitals, breasts, groin area, thighs, or buttocks directly or indirectly (over clothing) when it is clear that the other person does not invite it; unwanted vaginal or anal intercourse; incest; fellatio; cunnilingus; and penetration of the other person without permission.

This book is about cases involving physical sexual misconduct, not sexual harassment, and not rape in the usual understanding of the term. From this point on, the term *sexual misconduct* will refer to claims and accusations of various types of physical sexual acts other than those that fall into the category of rape.

Sexual misconduct generally involves a person in a position of trust, authority, or power who inflicts unwanted sexual activity on another person, with or without physical force. This is a book about the way linguistics can be used in sexual misconduct cases, not a book about the ways that the courts apply the law. Nevertheless, it is important to know something about the governing laws. As will be seen in the case descriptions that follow, the issues of consent, force, knowledge, ages of the participants, intent, and mutual agreement play an important role. These issues are dealt with specifically in the (1) U.S. federal statutes, (2) various state statutes (with the *Texas Penal Code* used as an example), and (3) the *Model Penal Code,* adopted in 1962. Prosecutions vary in which of these to follow.

1. U.S. FEDERAL STATUTES

The relevant parts of U.S. federal statutes relating to sexual misconduct are the following:

18 U.S.C. § 2241 Aggravated sexual abuse

(a) By Force of Threat.—Whoever, in the special maritime and territorial jurisdiction of the United States or in a Federal prison, or in any Federal department or agency, knowingly causes another person to engage in a sexual act—
  (1) by using force against that other person; or
  (2) by threatening or placing that other person in fear that any person will be subjected to death, serious bodily injury, or kidnapping;

  or attempts to do so, shall be fined under this title, imprisoned for any term of years of life, or both.

(b) By Other Means.—Whoever, in the special nature and territorial jurisdiction of the United States or in a Federal prison, or in any prison, institution, or facility in which persons are held in custody by direction of or pursuant to a contract or agreement with the head of any Federal department or agency, knowingly—

(1) renders another person unconscious and thereby engages in a sexual act with that other person; or

(2) administers to another person by force or threat of force, or without the knowledge or permission of that person, a drug, intoxicant, or other similar substance and thereby—

(A) substantially impairs the ability of that other person to appraise or control conduct; and

(B) engages in a sexual act with that other person; or attempts to do so, shall be fined under this title, imprisoned for any term of years or life, or both.

(c) With Children.—Whoever crosses a State line with intent to engage in a sexual act with a person who has not attained the age of 12 years, or in the special maritime and territorial jurisdiction of the United States or in a Federal prison, or in any prison, institution, or facility in which persons are held in custody by direction of or pursuant to a contract or agreement with the head of any Federal department or agency, knowingly engages in a sexual act with another person who has not attained the age of 12 years, or knowingly engages in a sexual act under the circumstances described in subsections (a) and (b) with another person who has attained the age of 12 years but has not attained the age of 16 years (and is at least 4 years younger than the person so engaging), or attempts to do so, shall be fined under this title and imprisoned for not less that 30 years or for life. If the defendant has previously been convicted of another Federal offense under this subsection, or of a State offense that would have been an offense under either such provision had the offense occurred in a Federal prison, unless the death penalty is imposed, the defendant shall be sentenced to life in prison.

(d) State of Mind or Proof Requirement.—In the prosecution under subsection (c) of this section, the Government need not prove that the defendant knew that the other person engaging in the sexual act had not attained the age of 12 years.

2. STATE STATUTES

State statutes vary slightly from federal law; although they are basically similar, sometimes state statutes are a bit more specific than the U.S. Code. The example given here is found in the *Texas Penal Code.*

§ 22.021

(1) If the person:

(A) intentionally or knowingly:

(i) causes the penetration of the anus or female sexual organ of another person by any means, without that person's consent;

(ii) causes the penetration of the mouth of another person by the sexual organ of the actor, without that person's consent; or

(iii) causes the sexual organ of another person, without that person's consent, to contact or penetrate the mouth, anus, or sexual organ of another person, including the actor; or

(iv) causes the sexual organ of a child to contact or penetrate the mouth, anus, or sexual organ of another person, including the actor; or

(v) [added September 1, 1997] causes the mouth of a child to contact the anus or sexual organ of another person, including the actor; and

(2) if:

(A) the person:

(i) causes serious bodily injury or attempts to cause the death of the victim of another person in the course of the same criminal episode;

(ii) by acts or words places the victim in fear that death, serious bodily injury, or kidnapping will be imminently inflicted on any person;

(iii) by acts or words occurring in the presence of the victim threatens to cause the death, serious bodily injury, or kidnapping of any person;

(iv) uses or exhibits a deadly weapon in the course of the same criminal episode; or

(v) acts in concert with another who engages in conduct described by subdivision (1) directed toward the same victim and occurring during the course of the same criminal episode;...

(B) the victim is younger than 14 years of age; or

(C) [added 9/1/95] the victim is 65 years of age or older.

3. THE MODEL PENAL CODE

Some jurisdictions follow the *Model Penal Code* (1985), especially the definitions of rape, deviate sexual intercourse by force or imposition, and sexual assault.

§ 213.1 Rape and Related Offenses

(1) Rape. A male who has sexual intercourse with a female not his wife is guilty of rape if:
  (a) he compels her to submit by force or by threat of imminent death, serious bodily injury, extreme pain or kidnapping, to be inflicted on anyone; or
  (b) he has substantially impaired her power to appraise or control her conduct by administering or employing without her knowledge, drugs, intoxicants or other means for the purpose of preventing resistance; or
  (c) the female is unconscious; or
  (d) the female is less than 10 years old.

Rape is a felony of the second degree unless (i) in the course thereof the actor inflicts serious bodily injury upon anyone, or (ii) the victim was not a voluntary social companion of the actor upon the occasion of the crime and had not previously permitted him sexual liberties, in which cases the offense is a felony of the first degree.

§ 213.2 Sexual Intercourse by Force or Its Equivalent.
A person who engages in deviate sexual intercourse with another person, or who causes another to engage in deviate sexual intercourse, commits a felony of the second degree if:

(A) he compels the other person to participate by force or by threat of imminent death, serious bodily injury, extreme pain or kidnapping, to be inflicted on anyone; or
(B) he has substantially impaired the other person's power to appraise or control his conduct, by administering or employing without the knowledge of the other person

drugs, intoxicants, or other means for the purpose of preventing resistance; or

(C) the other person is unconscious; or

(D) the other person is less than 10 years old.

§ 213.4 Sexual Assault

A person who has sexual contact with another not his spouse, or causes such other to have sexual conduct with him, is guilty of sexual assault, a misdemeanor, if:

(1) he knows that the contact is offensive to the other person; or

(2) he knows that the other person suffers from a mental disease or defect which renders him or her incapable of appraising the nature of his or her contact; or

(3) he knows that the other person is unaware that a sexual act is being committed; or

(4) the other person is less than 10 years old; or

(5) he has substantially impaired the other person's power to appraise or control his or her conduct, by administering or employing without the other person's knowledge drugs, intoxicants, or other means for the purpose of preventing resistance; or

(6) the other person is less than [16] years old and the actor is at least [four] years older than the other person; or

(7) the other person is less than 21 years old and the actor is his guardian or otherwise responsible for the general supervision of his welfare; or

(8) the other person is in custody of law or detained in a hospital or other institution and the actor has supervisory or disciplinary authority over him.

Sexual contact is any touching of the sexual or other intimate parts of the person for the purpose of arousing or gratifying sexual desire.

When most people hear the expression *sexual misconduct*, what immediately comes to their mind is rape. Sexual harassment in the workplace may also come to mind. Although rape, sexual harassment, and physical sexual misconduct are all covered under the term *sexual misconduct*, the focus in this book is primarily on physical sexual misconduct that does not meet the definition of rape. Yet there is overlap in many of the features, such as intention, perception, consent, coercion, and motive. For this reason, it seems useful to describe some of the legal aspects of both rape and sexual harassment.

RAPE

The most serious sexual misconduct offense (whether committed by males or females) is generally considered to be rape, now referred to as "sexual intercourse without consent" in many jurisdictions. This includes penetration by anything, including physical objects. In contrast, sexual assault is regarded as sexual intercourse without consent and without penetration, but it includes much more, such as any type of touching for sexual gratification.

Rape laws apparently began with William Blackstone's definition of rape as "carnal knowledge of a woman forcibly and against her will." For years the meaning of the force or threat accompanying rape was considered to be physical, but in 1975 *People v. Evans* (379 N.Y.S. 2d 912) added the defendant's intent and perceptions as the controlling factors. Some jurisdictions now also consider nonphysical coercion as force, although they require independent proof that such force was a factor, along with absence of consent. There has been considerable difficulty in finding agreement about what actually constitutes proof of force and lack of consent. For example, does lack of resistance indicate consent? If so, how much and what kind of resistance? After research studies made it clear that resisting rape was actually very dangerous for the victim, some states abolished the requirement of the victim's need to resist as proof of consent.

The issue of what constitutes consent also has been debated. Older definitions of rape contained no mens rea (mental state) requirements, but today consent or nonconsent is central to most rape cases. Of course, even this reasonable concept can be difficult to prove. What if the assailant held an honest but mistaken belief that the victim had consented? In some jurisdictions this is not an acceptable defense. Other jurisdictions debate about the way consent can be manifested and discovered, often based on the language that was reportedly used during the event and also about the way verbal exchanges about consent are treated at trial (Ehrlich 2001, 74 ff). Ehrlich points out the fallacy in the allegedly common-sense notion that women can resist unwanted sexual acts simply by offering direct and physical resistance, but this common-sense ideology overlooks the even more powerful role of fear. Even though rape was not charged, the question of consent played an important role in five of the cases described in this book.

Rape laws have come a long way from the common law doctrine, which considered a woman the property of her husband and merged her identity with his as soon a they were married, thereby considering marriage as an absolute consent to sex. Most U.S. jurisdictions have now abolished this doctrine and marital rape is now considered a crime.

SEXUAL HARASSMENT

Although the labels sexual harassment and sexual misconduct are somewhat related and are often used interchangeably, they are not quite the same things. Sexual misconduct that is deemed to fall into the category of sexual harassment does not necessarily include violent rape or unwanted physical sexual acts, but instead refers to wrongful sexual behaviors carried out by perpetrators who are usually associated with them in a workplace.

Sexual harassment includes a wide range of offensive behaviors that are found by law to be threatening and disturbing when a person in authority engages in various forms of sexual language or activity with a subordinate, such as a customer, client, student, or patient. Work supervisors, doctors, and teachers are the most common offenders, although other relationships are also possible. Allegations of sexual harassment sometimes can also lead to charges of sexual misconduct if a physical sexual act is involved.

Generally there are two types of sexual harassment in the workplace. One is the *quid pro quo* type, in which a person in authority requests sexual favors from an employee in exchange for a benefit, such as a raise in pay. Such harassment can also take a threatening tone when a promotion or pay increase or even loss of a job depends on whether the employee agrees to provide the sexual favor.

A second type of sexual harassment in the workplace is called the *hostile work environment*, which takes place in offices or other employment contexts. Examples include constantly telling dirty jokes, posting pornographic materials, using or allowing derogatory terms such "whore" or "bitch" to be used. This type of sexual harassment often includes intimidation, coercion, and bullying. The language may be intentionally directed to a single person or to a class of persons. It can be direct, as in language about a particular woman's physical attributes, or it can take the form of serious or semiserious proposals to engage in sexual relations. Such harassment may also be indirect, such as hanging photos of naked women in the workplace. It is usually not necessary to prove sexual harassment of bullying, intimidation, or coercion because sexual harassment is in itself bullying, intimidation, or, in the case of quid pro quo, coercion.

Sexual harassment laws have been in existence for several years. Although civil rights lawyers brought sexual harassment cases during the 1970s, more such lawsuits (usually against males, but occasionally also against females) began to be brought after a series of public interest events in the early 1990s, and most likely were stimulated by the October 1991 confirmation hearings concerning the nomination and eventual appointment of Clarence Thomas to the U.S. Supreme Court. This event pointed out the risks of bringing sexual harassment cases, but it also brought sexual harassment issues to the attention of most Americans. Robin Lakoff (2000, 120 ff) described the ensuing hearing that involved Anita Hill's accusation of harassment against Clarence Thomas as one of the decisive factors that helped turn the attention of the public to matters of sexual harassment. An almost contemporaneous incident that occurred during that period was the 1992 "Tailhook" investigation of male Navy aviators charged with indecent conduct toward female colleagues, followed by a series of sexual misconduct accusations against President Bill Clinton involving Gennifer Flowers, Paula Jones, and the most celebrated of all, Monica Lewinsky, all of which emphasized the role of asymmetrical power in the sexual arena. Lakoff observes, with considerable justification, that all of these events "had lasting effects on the cultural, as well as the sociopolitical climate" (2000, 155).

Two key cases were *Meritor Savings Bank v. Vincent* (477 U.S. 57) in 1986, which recognized hostile workplace harassment, and *Harris v. Forklift Systems, Inc.* (510 U.S. 17) in 1993, which clarified the reasonable person standard. Two Supreme Court decisions in 1998, *Burlington Industries v. Kimberly Ellerth* (542 U.S. 742) and *Farragher v. Boca Raton* (524 U.S. 775), followed by a 1999 decision in *Kolstad v. American Dental Association* (527 U.S. 526), more precisely defined the responsibilities of employers and workers in preventing sexual harassment in the workplace. America had finally discovered that the old "boys will be boys" attitude was far from satisfactory and acceptable.

Although given a boost by the events just mentioned, the idea of sexual harassment actually began with Title VII of the Civil Rights Act of 1964, which was enacted to prohibit discrimination of several types, including discrimination based on gender (discrimination against gays and lesbians has since been included). This act may have opened the door to lawsuits growing out of real or alleged sexual discrimination.

The term *sexual harassment* is relatively new to the lexicon. Peter Tiersma points out how legal vocabulary develops over the years: "Innovations in the law of contracts, torts, and damages has led to the coining of neologisms like *cramdown, hedonic damages, lost volume seller, palimony, sexual harassment, toxic tort,* and *wrongful birth*" (1999, 98). Perhaps because sexual harassment is still a relatively new legal concept, defining and implementing it has been somewhat slow in the workplace context.

Several explanations about the causes of sexual harassment have been offered by various disciplines such as sociology and psychology. One is what is called "the sexual spillover effect," which posits the cause as the function of innate male sexual desire. Although they are not sexual harassment cases, chapters 11 and 12 in this book relate to the sexual spillover effect. The second posited cause grows out of male and female social boundary differences about what constitutes acceptable sexual conduct. Chapters 5, 6, and 10 in this book relate to this explanation as well, although sexual harassment was not charged in any of them. A third explanation is the purported (and often unfortunately accurate) need by some males to create and maintain dominance over what they perceive to be subordinate females. It is not surprising that ninety percent of sexual harassment charges in the workplace, regardless of age, race, or socioeconomic level, are brought by women. Some believe that this is an unavoidable consequence of more and more women entering the workplace during the past half century or so.

Many companies and institutions now have established antiharassment policies and preventive procedures, but it remains difficult to provide clear and provable evidence to support or reject some harassment claims, largely because it can be hard to distinguish between presumably normal social interaction and harassment. Normal social interaction can be welcomed, but it is not welcomed when advances approach the level of sexual harassment. The same can be said about sexual misconduct affecting gays and lesbians.

PHYSICAL SEXUAL MISCONDUCT EXCLUDING RAPE

This type of sexual misconduct refers to intentional and premeditated wrongful, unlawful, and improper physical acts of a sexual nature. It includes an improper and unwelcomed sexual act that is defined by law as unlawful conduct motivated by the perpetrator's intentions and without regard to the consequences of the action. Like sexual harassment, sexual misconduct can also be committed by a person in a position of authority, but it goes beyond the minimum elements of harassment in that this person physically engages in some type of sexual activity with a subordinate, such as a patient, customer, student, or client.

Interestingly, while sexual harassment is implicitly illegal, sexual misconduct is not always automatically deemed illegal behavior. In some cases it can violate professional codes of ethics, even if the acts are welcome and consensual. But if the offended party believes that the sexual misconduct is unwelcome and not consensual, that party can file charges of sexual harassment as well as sexual misconduct.

PROVING SEXUAL MISCONDUCT

Unless a concurrent audiotape or videotape is made while sexual misconduct occurs, actual evidence of this crime is difficult to capture as it takes place. This is essentially the same problem facing law enforcement as it tries to capture language crimes such as bribery or money laundering (Shuy 1993, 2005). As a result, the evidence of unwelcome physical sexual activities often first takes the form of accusations by the alleged victims or witnesses, sometimes including reconstructed memories of past sexual events; police interviews with the victim, witnesses (if there are any), and the suspect; and in what has come to be called confrontation calls, in which victims make telephone calls to alleged perpetrators to try to get them to admit that they committed the past crime. In some cases confrontation meetings are arranged for the same purpose. Sometimes two or more of these strategies are used in the same case.

Victim-reported evidence

As in most cases where the evidence of past sexual misconduct crimes consists of illegal activity reported by alleged victims, these reports are often challenged by defense attorneys. They ask, for example, how we can know for sure what the accuser's intentions were? They challenge whether the offense actually happened or whether the accuser just thought it did. They suggest that the victim's motive was simply to get even with the person accused for some different real or imagined past offense. They wonder if the event could be interpreted in ways other than the way it was reported by the victim. When the only available evidence is self-reported, the defense will usually try to attack it. A substantiating witness to the same crime can improve the chances for the accusation to be sustained, but even when the self-reported evidence is substantiated by others, the same attack by the defense can be expected, in much the same ways.

Police interview evidence

Verification of the victim's accusation is usually the next step of law enforcement. Richard Leo (2008, 106–118) provides an excellent summary of the historical development of police interviewing in America. He describes the proper role of the intelligence gatherer as that of the collector of relevant case information in a neutral and dispassionate manner at the preadversary stage of the criminal process, noting, "when they act as partisans, they potentially undermine the three primary goals of the adversary system—the protection of legal rights, the control of government power, and the search for the truth—and thus risk contributing to unfair procedures and unreliable outcomes that may undermine the system's legitimacy" (Leo 2008, 19–20).

More will be said about the police interview in this book. For now, let it be clear that the police interview is a fact-finding exploration in which the interviewer's role is to be neutral and objective rather than subjective and accusatory. The goal of interviewing victims or witnesses is to gather their reported facts of the events, not to treat them as a sympathetic therapist might (Ceci and Bruck 1995; Poole and Lamb 2002). The goal is to gather the necessary facts in an objective and reliable manner. The goal is not to gather information subjectively by moving straight to the accusation phase without first gathering the necessary facts.

Police interrogation authorities urge and instruct law enforcement interviewers to follow the questioning model of first letting subjects narrate their own version of the event without interruption, followed by probes that use "wh" questions (who?, what?, when?, where?, why?), followed by yes–no questions. Tag questions ("Didn't you?") are not appropriate at any level. The point is to avoid the criticism of unduly influencing the suspect's responses.

Electronically recorded evidence

Realizing the potential weakness of self-reports and supporting witness accounts, law enforcement has developed the confrontation strategy, whether in telephone calls or arranged face-to-face meetings. After preparing the victim about how to manage such a call, the police sit next to the victim while he or she telephones the alleged perpetrator and engages in conversation that is intended to get the perpetrator to admit that he or she committed the offensive act. The confrontation call strategy is borrowed from law enforcement undercover operations that try to obtain admissions from alleged suspects in crimes such as business fraud, bribery, money laundering, and others (Shuy 1993, 2005). The victims are instructed to first let the suspects talk freely in the hope that they will admit the crime without further probing. If this strategy fails, the caller is instructed to drop hints suggesting the illegality of the past act in the hope that the person will bite on the vagueness or ambiguity of the hints and thereby incriminate him- or herself. If this strategy fails to elicit an admission, the caller is instructed to retell past events with or without being specific about their illegality, priming the pump a bit so that the suspect will discuss what happened and incriminate him- or herself in the process. If this strategy fails, the caller is instructed to make direct and unambiguous representations of the alleged past offensive acts, challenging the suspect to clearly and unambiguously admit or deny them.

Despite the logic of this four-step confrontation call strategy, confrontation callers tend to become impatient and skip step one entirely, failing to let the suspect talk and incriminate him- or herself. They also tend to omit step two (dropping hints that can lead to verification of the crime). Instead, they often move quickly to step three (the retelling of events strategy, coupled with considerable ambiguity) or even go straight to step four, the accusation phase.

In undercover operations using electronic equipment to gather evidence, it has been found that the most convincing, least challenged, and most acceptable evidence is the step one phase in which suspect incriminates him- or herself without a hint of external influence. When this happens, the defense cannot object that the undercover agent or the cooperating witness was suggestive or coercive. The more hinting, retelling of past events, or outright accusing that occurs, the farther away the investigator gets from the more useful self-report of guilt.

It is difficult for the defense to challenge clear admissions of guilt in criminal cases. However, undercover operations are not alone in realizing the advantage of self-generated admissions of guilt. The strategy also works very well in confrontation calls and meetings that are used in sexual misconduct cases.

Repressed (delayed and reconstructed) memory evidence

Perhaps the most controversial evidence of sexual misconduct is that which is based on traumatic, but allegedly suppressed, earlier memories (usually from childhood) that are then recalled much later, when the victim is an adult. Evidence of recalled memories that have been suppressed for many years are then pitted against the memories of the suspect, which are usually very different. An excellent review of the research on this issue has been published by Ceci and Bruck (1995, 187–251). When such cases first began to appear, the ability of adults to recall suppressed memories of childhood sexual abuse seemed to have some legal credence, but more recently such recall is now often seriously questioned. For one thing, the same motivation and interpretation concerns that underlie other types of self-reported evidence apply. Second, as Ceci and Bruck point out, the early research that appeared to support such accusations has become strongly disputed.

The police and the courts have to weigh these four types of evidence in any sexual misconduct case, whether it is spoken or written. The following chapters provide examples of how police and the prosecution make use of these techniques for gathering and using evidence in sexual misconduct cases.

SECTION I

Sexual Misconduct in the Workplace

In the previous chapter I pointed out that this book deals only with sexual misconduct cases in which physical sexual acts either took place, were alleged to have taken place at some time in the past, or were alleged to have been threatened or promised. It should be clear that this book does not include cases in which the conventional definition of sexual harassment occurs, nor does it include cases of alleged or actual rape.

Section I describes three cases that involve, to some degree, physical sexual misconduct in the context of the workplace, the setting in which most accusations of sexual harassment are brought. Even though the medical office is one of the common places where sexual harassment takes place, two physicians, Dr. Mark Berger (chapter 3) and Dr. Dillip Desai (chapter 4) were not charged with sexual harassment or rape. Instead, these doctors were charged with physical sexual misconduct.

The case of Sheriff William Preston (chapter 5) also took place in the context of the workplace, in this case the sheriff's own office. The location of the highly publicized case of former U.S. Senator Robert Packwood (chapter 6) took place in the workplace of his Senate office area.

[3]

FIGHTING OFF A QUID PRO QUO PROPOSITION

Even physicians have romantic inclinations, although ethically these aren't supposed to be expressed with their patients. In 1985 a woman named Candie suffered a serious closed head injury from an automobile accident. She filed a malpractice suit against her radiologist because she thought he had misdiagnosed her magnetic resonance imaging (MRI). This suit was dismissed because she did not provide an expert radiologist to counter the testimony of the defendant radiologist's interpretation of her MRI. In 1993 she continued to be unhappy with the defendant radiologist's interpretation and planed to appeal her case, but this time she hoped to get a competent radiologist to support her view. Toward this end, she paid a visit to Tucson, Arizona, neurologist Dr. David Rubin, who examined her and advised her that she did not have an acute medical problem. She was not pleased with this opinion because she wanted Dr. Rubin to produce an interpretation that would favor her in court. After he refused, she began calling him regularly, trying to get him to change his mind. He described her calls as "harangues filled with insults, epithets, accusations, and other vindictive comments." Finally he refused to have her as his patient, a fact that he recorded in his regular dictation.

Still distressed by this in 1993, Candie approached her primary care physician, Dr. Mark Berger, asking him to help her find another neurologist to counter the original radiologist's interpretation of the MRI and to support her appeal of her malpractice suit against the first radiologist. She reported that she wanted Dr. Berger to refer her to another neurologist who would be more positive about her case than Dr. Rubin was.

Candie called Dr. Berger, asking to see him in order to enlist his help. This call was not recorded, but she reported to the police that he asked her, "What's in it for me?" and she said that she responded, "Are you asking for sexual favors?" His answer, as she reports it, was, "You're a smart lady, figure it out and come see me tomorrow." After she recounted this to the police, they advised her to obtain a tape recording of her next conversation with the doctor. She went to his office the next day without an appointment, but with a small tape recorder hidden in her purse.

On November 4, 1993, she secretly recorded that visit with Dr. Berger. Then, a little over a month later, on December 14, 1993, she tape-recorded a second visit with Dr. Berger. Each visit lasted about half an hour. The fact that the police asked Candie to make a second tape recording is a strong indication that the evidence she collected in her first visit was not strong enough to bring about a prosecution.

Some readers may notice that the following presentation of the relevance of linguistics to the evidence data differs slightly from the way I usually present it. One of my most common and favored methods of showing my analysis to lawyers, judges, and juries is to produce charts showing the sequence of the individual topics introduced, the responses to those topics, the relevant speech acts used by participants, the conversational ambiguities, and conversational strategies, among others. However, this case was a little different, because the amount of data was relatively small. There were only two major participants, the differing agendas and schemas of the participants were relatively clear throughout, and the meanings of the words that were used (with one or two notable exceptions) were fairly clear.

As I considered these things, I decided to experiment by using a variation that is often used by modern literary critics, referred to as close reading, or as it is sometimes called, *explication de text.* Although this method is common in literary analysis, it actually harkens back to earlier scriptural commentaries of the Talmud, Islamic studies of the Koran, and other early religious analyses and explanations of the ostensible deep meanings in a text. Therefore, rather than setting out charts of individual topics and responses, I decided to cluster topic segments in each of the two conversations in a way that is similar to this close reading analysis.

VERBAL DUELING IN THE NOVEMBER 4 MEETING (FIRST CONVERSATION)

In her first recorded visit to Dr. Berger's office Candie brought with her some files relating to her appeal. The two went over these files while he asked her several times to describe her physical problems. Their conversation provides a fascinating duel about their separate conversational agendas. Candie was obviously trying to get Dr. Berger to agree to a quid pro quo. The quid was to convince him to write a letter to a neurologist he knew in order to convince him to assist her in her appeal. The quo was that he would receive sexual favors in exchange.

Dr. Berger, on the other hand, seemed perfectly willing to receive her sexual favors, but not unless these were disconnected from the quo of Candie's quid pro quo suggestion. He tried in vain to get her to say that she wanted sex with him willingly, with no association to her proposed quid. It should be made clear that a violation of doctor–patient ethics is not what this case is about, no matter how salient this matter might be to the medical board. This is a case about whether or not the doctor expressed a willingness to engage in illegal quid pro quo sexual misconduct in response to doing something of value for Candie. This was the only legal issue. In a way, it is similar to police stings of solicitation of prostitution. Here I provide partial transcripts of their entire first conversation on November 4, broken into larger topic segments.

Topic segment 1: Her request for a letter

MB: So you want me to uh, to more or less kind of help you out on this?

C: Not really. I don't want you to do anything unethical.

MB: Good. I'm not going to do anything like that. I just want the truth about the situation.

C: I want someone that understands the inner workings of this type of situation that I'm in, when they read the CAT scan wrong during the personal injury case where I was rear-ended and the CAT scan was interpreted incorrectly.

MB: What do you want me to do? You want me to say that I feel that they are being vague?

C: Yes.

This conversation begins with Candie's benign and perfectly appropriate request for him to write a letter that could help support her side of her malpractice case. Next, she gets more specific about what she wants.

Topic segment 2: The quid pro quo

MB: Alright. Let me write a letter telling them that I think they're being vague on this. And if I do that, then what? What's your... have you thought about it?

C: Thought about what? How we'd work that out? Well, I don't know what you're looking for. Does it cost money to get a report like this written? Is it unethical to do that?

MB: No, it's just putting me in a very, very vulnerable position with my colleagues.

C: What I want is a correct diagnosis. So what are we looking at exactly? What do you need? I mean, what can I give you?

MB: You said yesterday that you could come up with (unintelligible) and that's what you did.

C: Are we talking about sexual favors?

MB: Whatever you say. You tell me.

C: Are we?

MB: I don't know.

C: Mark, you gotta tell me where you're coming from. Are you talking about sexual favors? Are you?

MB: Do you feel that my writing you a letter is gonna help?

C: I don't know. It depends on your morals, Mark. I can find a way to go around these people if I need to. I'm sure I could take these films to somebody else.

MB: Okay. You're the boss. If you're comfortable, you're the boss. That's it. Okay. Let me know.

C: Let me know? I don't know what you're saying.

MB: Yeah, you know where I'm at.

C: 'Cause I don't know exactly what you want.

MB: Someone will find out.

Dr. Berger's vague question, "and if I do that, then what?" can be understood in three ways: (1) what good will my letter do in your law suit, (2) what is the legal process that will follow if I write the letter, or (3) the prosecution's interpretation, what do I personally get out of it? Although all three understandings are possible, the rest of this segment of the conversation tends to favor the prosecution's understanding.

Knowing that she needed to get Dr. Berger to say something specific and incriminating, Candie requested clarification: "So what are we looking at exactly? What can I give you?" The doctor's answer to this related to the medical forms she brought with her to their meeting. He answered that she told him she'd come up with them and she did. Recognizing that they were on different tracks, she ignored his reference to the forms and was, for the first time (on tape at least), explicit: "Are we talking about sexual favors?" This reprised her accusation to the police about their earlier untaped telephone call. The doctor replied, "Whatever you say, you tell me." Note that he gave neither a "no" nor a "yes" response. His agenda here and throughout was to try to get her to say that she would have sex with him willingly and unrelated to the pro quo that she was suggesting.

He quickly used the conversational strategy of returning to his safe haven topic, the letter he was being asked to write: "Do you feel that my writing a letter is gonna help?" To this, and probably recognizing that she needed to encourage the doctor's apparent interest in having sex with her, Candie coyly threatened that she could take the films to someone else, an action that would terminate her suggestion about his receiving any possible sexual favors. Having suggested this, she then reopened the sex topic by repeating that she doesn't know exactly what the doctor expects to receive for his cooperation in writing the letter. Apparently recognizing the danger of this as a quid pro quo, the doctor said, "someone will find out." This assumes that he knew she was after his explicit agreement to her suggested quid pro quo (writing a letter for sexual favors) but at the same time it provided his reason for not wanting to be exposed to it. Indirectly, he was explaining why he wouldn't utter the words she wanted to hear.

To this point, then, the verbal duel was a stalemate. He gave evidence of being interested in her sexual favors, but he wanted her to offer them outside of his agreement to write the letter, a statement she hadn't succeeded in getting him to make.

Topic segment 3: The doctor asks her what she wants

C: Well, I asked you what you wanted and you said no, so what else is there?

MB: Is that what *you want* to do?

C: No.

MB: Then why did you ask?

C: What would you think, have someone ask you that question that you asked me? I could think that—

MB: But you couldn't do it. Let me tell you something. You've got to stop. If you've got enough brain function to think about that. Look what you're doing (inaudible).

C: Well, Mark, I appreciate the time.

MB: It's my pleasure and you know what the truth is? I'm happy to help you if I can help you. I'll be right behind you to help you all the way, and I mean that seriously, but start a ruckus makes it more difficult than you think, okay? Isn't worth that. Okay?

C: I just thought maybe that you want more of a concrete, give me a break. It's hard to take my films down, especially when they look at it and they'll give public, there's so much work I mean. How do you work with the people that you're suing? Right? You don't.

MB: You have to know how to come back.

C: Because you tell me that you don't want any, you know.

MB: You know exactly what *you want*. You think about what *you want* and when you decide what *you want* to do (unintelligible).

C: But you said "no" to my question when I asked it.

MB: No I didn't. No, what I said was that's not necessarily, you're not *offering* anything like that yet. If that's not on the books, it's not on the books.

C: So I should think about that?

MB: Not unless you're *offering* it. If you're *offering* it, then you can think about it. If you're not offering it, then why think about it? It makes no sense.

C: I'm gonna make 'em do this. I'm an intelligent person. I know when they're taking me and these people have done a good job of taking me.

MB: Whatever *you want* to do. If you want me not to do it, I won't do it. If *you want* to do something for it, well that's fine, if *you want* to.

C: I'm gonna go for the appeal for sure, so you know that. I'm gonna go to the appellate court.

MB: Whatever *you want.* You're the boss.

C: I appreciate you doing that...I mean someone cares, you know?

MB: When you know what *you want* to do, let me know.

C: Okay.

Curiously, here Candie told the doctor that his previous answer to her suggestion about having sex was "no" and, even more curiously, that he had asked the very question that she had actually asked him earlier: "Are we talking about sexual favors?" Both statements are inaccurate. He had answered her question with neither "yes" nor "no" and it was she who suggested the quid pro quo of his letter in exchange for her sexual favors. He now responded, "Is that what you want to do?" most likely meaning, "do you *want* to give me sexual favors?"

It is clear that this verbal duel clearly boils down to whether she will tell him she'll give him sex willingly or whether, as she is indicating, it will be a quid pro quo arrangement. Again he didn't reply to the gist of her argument, now saying, "you've got to stop." What he wanted her to stop doing can be either to stop her court appeal or to stop trying to get him to accept her quid pro quo, most likely the latter.

Perhaps disappointed by her lack of success, Candie then threatened to leave, saying, "I appreciate the time," to which the doctor added, "start a ruckus makes it more difficult than you think. It isn't worth that." Now the word, "ruckus" can be interpreted two ways. His meaning appears to be that her suggested quid pro quo is not worth the danger it will bring to him. To this she first said, "I just thought that maybe you want to be more concrete." But she changed direction quickly and interpreted "ruckus" to mean her entire effort in her court appeal.

When things don't go the way we want them to go, one thing to do is to return to a safe haven topic, which is the conversational strategy Candie used here. When you find yourself out on a tree limb that is cracking, it's best to hurry back to the tree trunk. In this case, the indisputable safe haven was his letter relating to the court appeal. She talked about how hard it is to bring this case to trial and to work with the people she is suing. Oddly enough, the doctor had already agreed to help her by writing a letter, but she now held this up as something he is unwilling to do.

He encouraged her in her lament, saying, "You have to know how to come back," which must have seemed to her to crack open the door of sexual favors once more, so she said: "you tell me that you don't want any." He replied, "you know exactly what *you want*...think about what *you want* to do." His stress was on "you" and "want," emphasizing his effort to get her to separate her quid from her quo.

Not satisfied with this, Candie then introduced the topic that he had said "no" to her offer of sexual favors. He justifiably denied that he said "no," and explained, "you're not *offering* anything like that yet." She said, "so I should think about that?" and he responded, "Not unless you're *offering* it. If you're *offering* it, then you can think about it. If you're not offering it, then why think about it? It makes no sense."

Candie then returned once more to the safe haven topic of her court appeal, to which the doctor replied, "whatever *you want* to do. If *you want* me to not to do it, I won't do it. If you *want* to do something for it, well that's fine, if *you want* to." Candie then said she planned to go for an appeal. He replied, "whatever *you want*, you're the boss. When you know what *you want* to do, let me know," and the conversation ended.

Based on the recorded evidence of this conversation, the defense could not argue that the doctor did not want sexual favors, but it could clearly argue that the dueling speakers were not in agreement about the quid pro quo.

The prosecutors must have realized this, for they sent Candie back for a secretly recorded second conversation with the doctor on December 14, 1993. In cases where there are follow-up tapes, it is almost always the case that the government's intelligence analysis led them to understand that the first tape was not adequate to pursue a prosecution. In her second effort, we will see that Candie was even more explicit about what the doctor would get in exchange for his writing the letter.

VERBAL DUELING IN THE DECEMBER 14 CONVERSATION (SECOND CONVERSATION)

The second recorded conversation begins with a discussion of Dr. Rubin's letter in which he told Candie she was no longer his patient, an interruption by the doctor's secretary, and then:

Topic segment 1: Candie's vague requests for directive deflected

C: What do you want me to do?

MB: I'm not gonna go around on this again. All right?

C: Well, you have to be more specific with me, Mark.

MB: I went through this already. We don't wanna keep going around in circles.

C: Well, I'm ready to go forward. What do you wanna do? Do you wanna meet me somewhere? What do you wanna do?

MB: What do you wanna do? Uh, my letter, you want me to just send it to them?

The doctor ignored the by now already clear implications of her multiple requests for a directive and he quickly changed the topic back to his own safe haven, the letter, saying, "Do you want me to just send it to them? She said "yes" and he replied, "I could probably do it." Candie then returned to her major agenda.

Topic segment 2: Candie requests directives again

C: So where do we go from here?

MB: I don't know. *You tell me.*

C: Well, it's your play…you have to tell me or I don't know what you want, unless you tell me specifically what you want to do.

MB: If *you tell* me what *you'd* be willing to do, I'll tell you this sounds good to me. And we can make a deal.

C: You have to tell me, uh, where we are.

MB: That's it, that's it.

C: Well, I'm not gonna go on from here. I want you to write the letter.

MB: Okay.

C: And then what are we gonna do from there?

MB: Okay.

C: You have to let me know. Um, it's your stuff.

MB: Yeah.

C: So what do you wanna do after that? Do you wanna meet me here? I mean do you want a blowjob in the office? Do you wanna go to my house? Do you wanna go to a motel? What do you wanna do?

MB: Who exactly should I address the letter to?

CM: You didn't answer my question.

MB: Who should I address the letter to?

C: What do you want to do, Mark? Can we go in your office where no one will hear? What do you want to do?

MB: Maybe, maybe that'll be it.

C: Why don't we do that?

MB: All right. Anything bothering you?

After deflecting Candie's explicit offers of sexual favors, the doctor returned to his own safe haven of writing the letter. She persevered, however, suggesting that they move into his private office, to which he agreed.

The topic then shifted to Dr. Rubin's removing her as his patient for her intimidation and she then talked about trying to find a new neurologist. He warned her not to include all doctors in her condemnation because they are not all bad. After more discussion about the letter he is writing, she recycled her agenda topic once more.

Topic segment 3: Quid pro quo topic recycled

C: So what do you want to do?

MB: I'll write the letter.

C: Okay. And then what?

MB: Then we'll decide. We'll talk about it.

C: Well let's talk while I'm here. I can't be coming back and forth and back and forth. What do you want to do? Just let me know because we need to, I need to go forward irregardless.

MB: Okay. All right.

C: After you get the letter done and it's sent on the way, then what? Then what are we gonna do? We're gonna meet? You want to meet?

MB: That's fine.

C: Or what do you want to do?

MB: That's fine.

C: Do you want to meet at a motel or do you want to meet here?

MB: Either way. We'll decide. You name the place.

C: How about next week?

MB: What day?

C: Monday or Tuesday.

MB: Where at?

C: Here.

MB: Sure.

C: During business hours?

MB: How about calling me? We'll decide.

C: I've never asked you for anything.

MB: I won't do anything I don't want to do. Keep that in mind. Okay? Do you do anything you don't *want* to do?

C: But you want something in return for that?

MB: I don't want to put you in a corner that way. That's not something, if you feel real bad about that, then I don't want that. I mean, if that's easy and that's a piece of cake and that's no big deal, then cool.

C: How do you think I fucking feel?
MB: I don't know. Tell me.

Candie again recycled her topic to get the doctor to tell her that he'll write the letter for her sexual favors. It was "fine" with him to meet, either at a motel or at his office, then he decided on his office. He appeared to suspect that she was taping their conversation and asked her to call him back. The doctor continues his repetition drill with the word "want." Interestingly, the doctor reversed her point of his wanting sex by placing the decision on her ("I don't want to put *you* in a corner that way"). She was beginning to be frustrated and angry at her inability to get him to say the magic words.

Topic segment 4: Denials by both

MB: Don't do anything that you're not comfortable with doing in regards to everything. Don't.
C: And you'll write the letter for me anyway? If I say no, you'll write the letter?
MB: I could write the letter saying that I don't agree with some of the, I can generally do what you want.
C: But if I don't sleep with you, then that's different.
MB: I didn't say that. You just said that. I never said that. No, it's different. That's absolutely not true. Is there anything else we need to talk about?
CM: Well I guess not.
MB: Just, I'll try and help you for nothing.
C: Now it's for nothing. You're gonna change your mind?
MB: You make me feel like I'm doing the wrong thing and I don't want to feel that way.
C: Don't you feel like you're doing the wrong thing anyway?
MB: By writing the letter?

C: No, by asking me to have sex.

MB: No. I didn't ask that. You *offered* that. I didn't ask that.

C: I want you to stay away from me.

MB: Okay, but I won't write the letter.

C: If you don't write the letter, I'll get someone else to write the letter.

MB: Okay. Don't be angry with me. I've never done anything to hurt you ever. I'm only trying to help. The door's open.

C: Kiss my ass. Write your fucking letter and let me sign.

MB: Okay, but you've gotta be nice to me. You call me when you're ready to be nice.

C: Make up your fucking mind. Okay, I'm out of here.

MB: Okay. Good-bye.

The conversation ended with neither of them getting what they wanted, not even about the letter in question. Her major reason for asking him to write it was to use this as her quid pro quo. In the end, it was not even clear that the letter would be written. At any rate, Candie failed to get the doctor to say that he'd write the letter in exchange for sex with her. He certainly gave every appearance of wanting sex with her, but not as a quid pro quo. She had to want to do it. He clearly wanted to have sex with her, but sex that was disassociated from writing the letter.

These two conversations are classic examples of participants having separate agendas and then verbally dueling with each other about how to get the other person to agree. Candie was the intelligence gatherer, no doubt assisted by law enforcement, and the prosecutor was the intelligence analyst. The job of the intelligence analyst is to weigh the evidence gathered by the intelligence gatherer and determine whether it is strong enough to support the charges, in this case the charge of sexual misconduct.

It is of little consequence to the legal case that the doctor really wanted to have sex with his patient. Candie certainly suggested sex in these conversations and the doctor did not reject the possibility, but this is a matter for the medical board of ethics to deal with, not the courts. The legal question is whether he accepted Candie's suggestion as a quid pro quo for his writing a letter in support of her legal appeal. He was certainly willing to write the letter, for which there is no legal restriction. He also was consistent in rejecting her suggestion that he could have sex with her as a quid pro quo payment for this action. Even in segment 4 of the second tape, when he agreed to meet with her in his office, he had not agreed to do this as payment for sex. He invited her to call him when she was ready to "be nice," which was not connected with his writing the letter, to his way of thinking at least.

AGENDA AND SPEECH ACTS

The participants in this case had frequently recycled but very opposite agendas—her quid pro quo for sexual favors versus his insistence that she willingly give him sex—and they consistently produced language evidence of their positions about this. Candie provided many examples of the speech acts of requesting information, requesting clarification, and requesting directives. The doctor offered her advice at least one time ("think what you want to do") and both denied the other repeatedly. Candie also accused the doctor of saying something that he clearly did not say. She also threatened to get someone else to provide what she wanted.

SAFE HAVEN CONVERSATIONAL STRATEGY

Both of them retreated to their safe haven topics whenever it appeared that they were getting nowhere with their own agendas. Dr. Berger offered to write the letter and Candie indirectly offered to provide sex to him if he would only say this. Their verbal duels started and ended with a stalemate. The important concept of consent in sexual misconduct cases cannot be found in these conversations.

INTELLIGENCE ANALYSIS

Should the prosecutor have brought charges against the doctor for sexual misconduct? To do so, the prosecutor would have needed to find verbal evidence from the tapes that this was the doctor's intention. Such evidence is simply not there. Their conversations may give the appearance that a quid pro quo was agreed upon, but such an appearance was disproved by the actual language evidence, once it was examined carefully. And because the doctor engaged in ethically questionable practice does not mean that he engaged in a legal crime. Whether or not the prosecutor was influenced by this, his intelligence analysis was not adequate here.

[4]

A PATIENT CONFUSES HER DOCTOR

In October 1993 a criminal lawyer in an Alabama city asked me to assist him in a case involving a local gynecologist, Dr. Dillip Desai, who had been indicted on one count of forcible oral sodomy and one count of sexual battery. One of his patients, Angela Rediatu, a twenty-six-year-old woman born in Ghana but now living in that city, had received an abortion from the doctor a couple years earlier. Now she returned to his office again, but this time she accused him of sexually assaulting her while she was under sedation. The physical evidence in this case consisted of six recorded telephone calls made by this patient to Dr. Desai at his office. She tape-recorded four calls on her own and then took them to the police as proof of her accusation. To the police, these calls appeared to link the doctor romantically with her but lacked clear evidence that he actually committed any sexual misconduct, so they asked her make a fifth call to try to get the doctor to admit committing oral sodomy. With police guidance she made the call. After they still found a lack of inculpatory clarity, the police had her make a sixth and final call. After this call the prosecutor was apparently satisfied and he subsequently filed sexual misconduct charges against Dr. Desai.

Since suspects in successful confrontation calls often reveal their agendas, use various speech acts, and make references to specific issues, I decided to use these tools as the starting points for my analysis. What were both of the participants' conversational agendas? How were promises, agreements, directives, requests for directives, apologies, or denials made? Were the speakers always referring to the same things? The linguistically untrained listener can often spot misunderstood references, but it's easy for them to be fooled by whether or not things are as clear and felicitous as they first appear.

TOPICS AND AGENDAS

It was obvious from the start that Mrs. Rediatu's conversational agenda was to get Dr. Desai to give her advice about how to deal with her husband, to acknowledge the doctor's past actions and apologize for them, and to accuse the doctor of performing oral sex with her. She dominates their conversations, introducing twice as many topics as Dr. Desai's (her fifty-nine to his twenty-nine). The person who introduces the majority of topics often tends to control the conversation. The doctor's topics are efforts to calm her down, to try to determine what her problem was, and finally to dismiss her calls with promises to call her back later, at a time when he was not so busy with his patients.

SEEKING AN ADMISSION AND APOLOGY

Aside from these tape-recorded telephone conversations, the only evidence of a crime was her unverified testimony. The police apparently believed that if the tapes showed his admission and apology, her case would be very strong. If Dr. Desai did not admit and apologize for the things she accused him of, he had a chance of escaping conviction. As is often the case, everything depended on the language used and how it could be understood by the participants and, of course, by later listeners, such as the police, prosecutor, judge, and jury.

EXTERNAL CONTEXT

All law cases occur in a social context, and this one held some particular difficulties for the doctor. One issue external to the case was that he provided abortions in an especially conservative state where such practices were frowned upon. Another issue was that it was widely known that a few years earlier he had been charged with disposing of aborted fetuses by burning them in a nearby empty field. If these external context issues weren't enough to influence the jurors, the doctor had additional jury perception problems as well, because during his trial two other female patients came forth and reported that he had sexually assaulted them in the same way.

Dr. Desai's defense attorney had a steep hill to climb. But the state's only physical evidence consisted of those six tape-recorded conversations that were expected to be central to the verdict. The extent to which jurors consider past bad acts, whether they are instructed to ignore them or not, is always difficult to determine.

BACKGROUND EVENTS

An incident that took place shortly before she taped these conversations is also important. After an early visit to the doctor, Mrs. Rediatu left his office and waited in the parking lot for him to leave work. As he walked to his car, he asked her what she was doing there and she replied that she had no money for bus fare to get home. He then volunteered to drive her home, and on the way there she asked him to stop at a fast food restaurant where she ordered some hamburgers. He waited in his car, and after she bought the food, he discovered that they were only a block or so away from where she lived. As harmless as his act of kindness may seem, it later played a role in his prosecution, because she used this event as an indication that she had a romantic connection with him. In addition, getting him to stop for food so close to her home provided the opportunity for local people to see them together.

HER VISIT TO THE DOCTOR

When Mrs. Rediatu came to the doctor this time, she said she thought she was pregnant again. When Dr. Desai had performed an abortion on her a few years earlier, she never told her husband about it. He thought she had simply miscarried. She told the doctor that she now needed an excuse about her current visit to see him, because, if it turned out that she was pregnant again, her husband would never approve of an abortion.

The audio quality of the six tapes was poor and the accents of both speakers did not contribute to their clarity. Dr. Desai's speech had slight traces of his Pakistani upbringing, and even though English is also the official language of Ghana, where Mrs. Rediatu grew up, she spoke with an accented version of English and there was ample evidence that her first language influenced her speech. This may have been why the prosecution's transcript was inaccurate in many places. The linguist's first priority is to prepare a corrected transcript that can be used subsequently at trial. Space limitations do not allow for entire transcripts here, but the segments analyzed will provide a relatively clear picture of the major parts of the conversations.

THREE CONVERSATIONAL STRATEGIES

Mrs. Rediatu employed three conversational strategies in her effort to elicit an admission of guilt from Dr. Desai. At first she tried to get the doctor to self-generate his own guilt by describing the accusations that her husband had been making about her behavior. This follows the technique used in police interrogations when the officer lets the suspect talk himself into jail. This yielded nothing incriminating. Her second strategy was to ask the doctor what she should do about her situation. Her reasoning here was that if the doctor gave her directives, this could implicate him. This too yielded nothing that proved his guilt. Finally, her third strategy was to elicit the doctor's apology.

Strategy 1: Describing her husband's accusations about her (calls 1–4)

In the first four conversations that Mrs. Rediatu tape-recorded on her own, she reports only her husband's accusations about her alleged romance with Dr. Desai. In the following excerpts of their conversations in calls 1 and 4, Mrs. Rediatu tries to get Dr. Desai to say that if her husband leaves her, Dr. Desai will be her next lover.

Mrs. Rediatu's call 1 topics:

- He [her husband] thinks that there's something fishy going on.
- He keeps pressuring me that there is something between the two of us.
- He said he's going to take you to the police station if I don't tell him the truth.
- He says, "I am in love with somebody." He is putting pressure on me to tell him.

Mrs. Rediatu's call 4 topics:

- He felt you did something to me.
- He started saying I am dating you.
- This time he thinks I did something.

Interspersed in call 4, Mrs. Rediatu added:

- Why should I suffer because of somebody?
- I am trying to pretend nothing happened.
- I feel somebody told him something about a guy.
- I can't keep pretending nothing happened.

Mrs. Rediatu's speech acts, in particular her accusations, her attempts to get Dr. Desai to acknowledge what she claimed he did, and her requests for the doctor to give her directives are treated first here. The following charts show not only her speech acts, but also the doctor's responses to those speech acts.

Strategy 2: Her requests for directives (calls 1, 3, and 4)

Mrs. Rediatu	**Dr. Desai's response**
Call 1:	
"What do I say? What do I tell him?"	
	"Well, you might have miscarried, you know."

"What do you want me to tell him?"	
	"Well just tell him that you started bleeding, you know, that's all."
"So when he asks me about any, why I was in your hospital and I was dizzy, what do I tell him?"	
	"Nothing, you know, except you never came here, that's all, right?"
Call 3:	
"He said I was talking to you yesterday."	
	"You just tell him that you had a pain and that's why you were calling."
"If he gets back to me, what do I do?"	
	"Okay, let me, I will call you back, okay?"
Call 4:	
"What do you expect me to tell him?"	
	"You tell me."

"He wants me to get out of the house. Where do I go?"

"Listen, if you have problems, then you tell me, I will go out and make an arrangement for you to stay. Okay?"

(*crying*) "I mean just tell me what you want me to do because when he comes home" (*she then changes her own subject*).

"If you will keep crying, I cannot listen to you."

"When my husband leaves me, you will not be ready for me, is that right?"

"Why should I be?"

The doctor tried to provide answers to her fear that her husband might ask her about her abortion. He even suggested that she lie to her husband about why she came to him for medical attention. His suggestion for her to lie, of course, did not play well for him. The prosecutor made much of the fact that if Dr. Desai could suggest that she lie about this, why wouldn't he tell her to lie about other matters, or even worse yet, why wouldn't he lie about his own involvement in the case. Richard Leo points out that detectives are trained that if they can't elicit a confession, they should try to catch the suspect in a lie. He cites the words of one detective, who told him "a lot of times a good lie is just as valuable and good as a confession because all you need to do is just show that one aspect of what he said, and the jury is not going to believe anything the defendant says" (Leo 2008, 23).

Up to the time she asked him if he was "ready for her," the doctor gave evidence of his own schema, which was that she was concerned about telling her husband about her earlier abortion and the fact that she was now pregnant again. Dr. Desai's final response indicated that he was now catching on to her schema about what this conversation was really all about—getting him to become her next lover or mate.

Strategy 3: Her request for an apology (calls 5 and 6)

Interestingly, she did not directly accuse the doctor of anything in calls 1 and 2. Instead, both calls focused on Mrs. Rediatu's reports of her husband's accusations about her. Since calls 3 and 4, also made without police supervision, did not explicitly link the doctor with sexual misconduct, the police instructed Mrs. Rediatu to convey her accusations directly to him in calls 5 and 6. These included several recycled requests for his apology:

- I thought you were going to say you were sorry for what happened.
- Are you sorry for what you did to me?
- Apologize to me for what you did to me that night, for not putting your prick in my mouth.
- Are you sorry for putting your prick in my mouth?
- Are you sorry for that?
- You are sorry for what happened that night?
- Just say you are sorry for what happened that night.
- I ask you if you are sorry for what you did to me.
- Are you sorry for what happened?

Mrs. Rediatu apparently believed she had elicited an acknowledgement from the doctor during her first four calls, but it was clear that she had only confused the event of her abortion of a couple years ago with the current incident. Call 1 was made the day after the doctor had seen Mrs. Rediatu, who thought she was pregnant again and was complaining about bleeding. As noted above, he had driven her home after that appointment. Now the doctor has several patients waiting in his office. She made her accusation at the very beginning of her call. Confusingly, she said that the doctor did not let her do the sex act that he is accused of in the indictment. Notice that immediately after saying this, she changed the subject to his anger about this. This is the "hit and run strategy" (Shuy 2005). He responded to her changed topic, saying he was not angry with her. Here, and throughout the six calls, he was clearly trying to get rid of her annoying phone calls.

She quickly changed the subject to the fact that she did not tell her husband about the abortion she had a couple years earlier. The doctor agreed that it would not be good for her to tell her husband about that. She then rapidly changed the subject to her husband's suspicion that she was dating the doctor. He responded that she came to his office because she was bleeding and agreed with her that she is "innocent." She then began crying and moved to the next accusatory step, that they were alone in his office, that her husband will leave her, and that the doctor will not be ready for her.

Mrs. Rediatu then changed what she expected the doctor to be sorry for by reprising her previous abortion, saying that the doctor should be sorry for not insisting that her husband be with her when she had that abortion. He responded that he's sorry about that. This is by no means a felicitous apology for having sex with her. It is, by her own definition, his statement about being sorry that he didn't insist that her husband be present for her abortion.

The police obviously were not satisfied with the four initial phone calls that Mrs. Rediatu brought to them. They subsequently asked her make another call, and then still another. By the sixth call, in which the police thought they had the necessary confession, Dr. Desai had grown very weary of speaking with Mrs. Rediatu and tried very hard to end the call.

Mrs. Rediatu's requests for an apology constituted her third and last conversational strategy for eliciting the doctor's guilt. Having failed to elicit self-generated guilt and having failed to get him to implicate himself by telling her what to do or say, she tried to elicit an apology in the last two conversations. In all, she requested his apology thirteen times. The fact that she did this repeatedly is evidence that she (or the monitoring police officer) was not satisfied with Dr. Desai's responses, for if she had received a guilt-producing response, there would have been no need to tape-record further.

In one of her last requests for an apology, Mrs. Rediatu explicitly states, "I don't know why you are sorry," indicating that even to her it was not clear what Dr. Desai's "I'm sorry" referred to. In this, she is quite accurate, for the doctor had expressed his regrets earlier only for not having insisted that her husband accompany her to his office, for what "he did to her" (although he was not specific what "did" refers to in this passage), and that she "feels like that."

The first five calls did not provide the prosecutor with what he believed he needed, but the last call seemed conclusive enough for him to bring charges of sexual misconduct. Mrs. Rediatu was finally specific and the doctor's responses seemed to implicate him:

Call 6

Mrs. Rediatu	Dr. Desai's response
I just want you to apologize to me.	
	For what?
For what you did to me that night.	
	Okay.

For putting your prick in my mouth
while I was sleeping. Yes, that's what
I wanted to apologize and I will leave
you alone.

Okay, I'm sorry, okay? I am
busy right now.

Tell me "I'm sorry" and just tell me
something now that just makes up,
I feel I should forgive you and don't
talk about it again.

Okay, I'm sorry, okay?

Sorry for putting your prick in my
mouth whilst I was sleeping, and
you're sure?

Okay, I'm sorry if you feel
like that.

Are you sorry for that? Just say yes or
no and...

I told you already I'd...

...that you are sorry for what hap-
pened that night? Yes or no? You say
you are sorry and I don't know why
you are sorry and I'm asking, is that
for what happened that night? That's
why you're sorry?

I will talk to you later.

Yes, I am sorry, okay? I am
busy right now.

No, just say you are sorry for that. I'm asking you are you sorry for what happened that night? Say yes or no.	
	Okay, you come see me and then we will talk.
So you are not sorry?	
	I know you feel bad and I'm sorry but you don't understand so...
I ask you if you are sorry for what you did to me and you say just leave you alone and we'll be friends.	
	Okay, I already told you, okay?
That you are sorry for what happened?	
	Okay. Bye.

The doctor said, "Okay, I'm sorry, okay? I am busy right now" after Mrs. Rediatu said "for putting your prick in my mouth." Although this would seem to be what the prosecutor was waiting to hear, Mrs. Rediatu was apparently urged by her police handler to probe further, possibly because the doctor's two "okays" along with his "I am busy right now" suggested that he would say anything to get rid of the call. Since it is typical for the police to coach and sit with alleged victims when they make confrontation calls, the handler sitting with Mrs. Rediatu apparently prompted her to repeat her question, which she did, saying, "Sorry for putting your prick in my mouth?" His answer to this repeated question is even less satisfactory than his first response, because now he clearly reduced his apology to "I'm sorry *if you feel* like that." Being sorry about how a person feels is not a felicitous apology for an alleged offense.

Mrs. Rediatu appeared to understand the doctor's vagueness, but her follow-up questions were not nearly as specific as her first one, as she asked, "sorry for *that*?" and "sorry for *what happened*?" Both references are too ambiguous to produce felicitous apologies. She even admitted that she still didn't know what the doctor was sorry about. By now, the doctor's patience has worn thin. He dismisses her with a pre-close saying, "come see me and then we'll talk" and finally, he simply ends the conversation. The prosecutor apparently was more convinced that the doctor had apologized for the offense than Mrs. Rediatu was, for he indicted him anyway.

This appears to be a case of a doctor getting too involved in the private life of his patient. In conversations in which one of the participants is irrational or hysterical, the calmer participant, especially the superordinate one, usually tries to calm the other person in whatever way possible. As anyone who has been in such a situation can attest, it is common to urge an excited person to calm down, to make some kind of promises, even vague ones, whether or not there is any intent to keep them, and finally, to say whatever the overly excited person seems to want to hear, just to end the conversation. When there is ambiguity in the accusations, when there are denials and requests for directives made by the excited party, when the caller displays illogicality and utters contradictory statements, and when the calmer participant eventually becomes frustrated, conversations can become disjointed, taking on different meanings to the different participants. This appeared to be what happened in this case.

[5]

THE SHERIFF WHO DIDN'T KNOW WHAT HIT HIM

Sometimes even law enforcement officers get tangled up in sexual misconduct cases. In 1998 the sheriff of a South Carolina town was one of them. Sheriff William Preston, then seventy-one years old, had spent his last forty-five years in law enforcement and no allegations of any type of wrongdoing had ever been brought against him. But he now found himself on the other side of the law, with misdemeanor charges of indecent exposure and assault and battery brought against him in his very own jurisdiction.

Sheriff Preston's problems began when a secretary who worked in another department made these accusations to the district attorney. After receiving the woman's complaints, the state police were brought in to install audio and video recording devices in the complainant's work area in order to gather sexual misconduct evidence against the sheriff. The video portion of the ten-minute recording failed to function at all and the audio track was very difficult to hear. At the same time, however, the woman also recorded the conversation with a microcassette recorder hidden in her purse. Her recorder was voice activated and therefore it cut in and out throughout the conversation she taped with the sheriff. Both the Federal Bureau of Investigation (FBI) and a forensic audio analyst hired by the defense tried to enhance the quality of the tapes, but with little success. The defense analyst reported that the microcassette recorder's voice activation control periodically malfunctioned and shut itself off. Despite these troublesome technical problems, both the prosecution and defense prepared transcripts of what they believed to be the crucial portions of the brief tape recording, leading to considerable disagreement about what was said.

SCHEMAS

It is always useful to begin work on such cases with as clear a notion as possible about the schemas of the participants. It is often difficult to know these with certainty, of course, but the most likely one for the sheriff was that he was trying to find some romantic spark in his life. Based on what he said, he probably misunderstood the woman's signals and thought he might move their friendship to the next level. He had no record of sexual misconduct behavior in the past and he had no reported reputation as a lecher. It is less clear what the woman's schema was. It could be that she was offended by the sheriff's romantic moves and justifiably complained to the police. Alternatively, she could have been motivated by colleagues in the office to get rid of Preston by bringing a sexual misconduct misdemeanor charge against him.

Shortly before this, however, Williams had received an anonymous and undated letter warning him that "some people," including a police captain, "were after him" because the captain wanted to replace Preston as sheriff. This letter, hand-printed in block letters, claimed that one of his captains was trying to make a case against the sheriff for personal and political reasons. Preston's lawyers could not provide the necessary writing samples of other suspects to compare them as possible authors, so there was no way to identify the author of this letter. Thus it turned out to be useless for both sides in the case. On the surface, however, it appeared to have been written by an older male Caucasian (probably older than fifty), with a high school education at most. There were also a few clues that suggested the writer was involved in law enforcement work. This led me to question whether the letter might have been written by Sheriff Preston himself. If so, it might not work well in his defense. Because of this possibility, the defense lawyer decided not to use the anonymous letter as evidence and he had to abandon the theory that the charges were politically motivated. That left him with only the woman's accusation, and in order for the prosecution to succeed, proof of her accusation would depend on what was on the confrontation tape.

EXTERNAL CONTEXT

Another consideration in this case was that the sheriff was very hard of hearing, as his contemporaneous audiology report, placed in evidence by his attorney, indicated. If the suspect cannot hear what the accused is saying, the oral evidence can be at least questionable. I have worked on other cases where the defendant simply couldn't hear what the accuser was saying (Shuy 1993, 85–99).

A PRECEDING UNRECORDED CONVERSATION

Conversations such as the one used in evidence here take place in an ongoing context. Things said in previous conversations have a way of explaining vagueness and ambiguity in the evidence conversation. For example, on the day preceding this recorded conversation, the sheriff told the woman that he had just learned of her complaint, and he testified later that he confronted her about it in a conversation that was not recorded. On the following day, as noted above, the video operated effectively, but the audio portion did not. The videotape was not useful to either side, except that both the woman and the sheriff appeared to be calm and they displayed no animated nonverbal excitement. Since their nonverbal behavior wasn't useful to the prosecutor, he didn't include that videotape as evidence. This left the prosecutor with only the relatively scratchy and sometimes unclear backup microcassette audiotape that the woman had recorded inside her purse.

THE TAPE RECORDING AND TRANSCRIPT

Since this recorded conversation is so brief, it is possible to show the entire transcript here. Notice that the end of the tape includes an inadvertently recorded brief exchange between the woman and an unidentified male agent. When the tape recorder remains in operation at the ends of conversations after the targets are gone, sometimes the analyst can find useful information there. In this case, this last exchange proved very helpful to the defense.

WOMAN: Uh, I want to ask you about something confidential.

SHERIFF: Okay. Hey Jim (*speaking to a man who walked by*). She wants to tell me something. You mind going down to the other end of the hall?

JIM: No sir, I don't mind.

WOMAN: I kinda decided I want to get this out in the open.

SHERIFF: Huh?

WOMAN: I want to get this out in the open just in case she talks to you.

SHERIFF: Uh-huh.

WOMAN: Uh, because, you know, I had told her, you know, what you did that day, you know, you had pulled your penis out and all that stuff, talk about that.

SHERIFF: Huh?

WOMAN: I said I hated talking about that.

SHERIFF: Uh-huh.

WOMAN: And, uh, and then, you know, I had told her, remember when I had a pain in my side?

SHERIFF: Un-huh.

WOMAN: And then you wanted to feel it and then you went down my pants and you were feeling (inaudible), uh, you know, I mean...

SHERIFF: So what did she have to say?

WOMAN: Well, I just told her I wanted somebody to talk to. I didn't want to put her through anything.

SHERIFF: Uh-huh.

WOMAN: And, uh, I mean, hopefully she can keep it hush-hush.

SHERIFF: Uh.

WOMAN: So I just wanted you to know.

SHERIFF: Okay. It will not happen anymore.

WOMAN: Okay, I, I thank you for that because, I mean, you know, that scared me.

SHERIFF: There's not gonna be, you know, you know we'd been carrying on and carrying on and I took it the wrong way I think.

WOMAN: Well see, I didn't, that's why I didn't tell the girls over there because I didn't want it to get back to you, you know, I mean, I knew that they would tell you and, but I had to have somebody to talk to and...

SHERIFF: Okay, everything's fine as long as you don't want to testify. That's just fine because it will never happen again, I assure you.

WOMAN: Because I, you know, that's fine. Scared about it.

SHERIFF: Because I think the world of you and I guarantee it will not happen.

WOMAN: Okay, because I was, you know, scared with, you know, last night, you know, after we talked about it. I didn't even know that letter came to you and, and it scared me so bad last night that I said, oh gosh, I said, you know, I just didn't want this to get back.

SHERIFF: Just play it cool and if she says any more to you and you say you don't want to testify to it and I'll assure you it will not happen again.

WOMAN: Okay. Well, I mean does Nancy know or?

SHERIFF: Huh?

WOMAN: Does Nancy know?

SHERIFF: No, and I'm not going to tell her anything.

WOMAN: Okay. I see what it, good too, you know.

SHERIFF: Yeah, I won't tell anything to her. I'm not going to say anything to nobody to tell you the truth.

WOMAN: I mean, good. You didn't tell Charlene?

SHERIFF: Oh, hell no.

WOMAN: Good. Okay.

SHERIFF: I didn't tell a damn soul.

WOMAN: Oh, good.

SHERIFF: Okay, dear.

WOMAN: I just didn't want anybody just badgering me and…

SHERIFF: Nobody's going to bother you, and me either. And the main thing is I don't want it to get out and you don't either. It would be bad for both of us as far as that goes.

WOMAN: Yeah, I know. That's what I say.

SHERIFF: Look, I appreciate it.

WOMAN: Well, you're welcome.

SHERIFF: Thank you dear.

WOMAN: Thank you. Thank you for promising me not to do it again (laughs), but I should have talked to you about this.
SHERIFF: Okay.
WOMAN: Thanks.

At this point the conversation between the sheriff and the woman ended, but the microphone was still on, picking up her conversation with an unidentified male agent who was monitoring the event nearby.

WOMAN: (inaudible) I know, I mean, you know, I really didn't have a lot to say, you know, but you've already recorded (laughs). Oh I know, I was sitting there going…
UNIDENTIFIED MALE AGENT: Couldn't figure it out (laughs). Couldn't figure out what you (laughs)…
WOMAN: No he couldn't. He couldn't figure out what I wanted to talk to him about but, 'cause I wind up talking to (inaudible).

Even though both the agent and the woman agreed that the sheriff never figured out what their conversation was all about, the prosecutor believed the sheriff had confessed to the crime for which he was accused. But is this true? Wrightsman and Kassin (1993, 95) illustrate how a questioner can manipulate uncertainty, interpersonal trust, and expectation in order to make these three aspects of the situation alter the person's susceptibility to suggestions.

SCHEMA UNCERTAINTY AND AMBIGUITY

Prime candidates for maintaining different schemas while appearing to be in agreement are our old friends vagueness and ambiguity, for these meet the criterion of uncertainty head-on. If the participants have different schemas that guide what they are talking about, the need for specificity increases in order to meet the requirement of mutual understanding. In this conversation the uncertainty of choice includes the ambiguous uses of "this," "that," "it," "what," "she," and "her." If we didn't know in advance that the woman had first talked to another female friend about the issue, we wouldn't know who the "she" and "her" referred to. But during the discovery process this was made clear. In contrast, her references to "this" and "what" were unclear to the sheriff:

> WOMAN: I want to get *this* out in the open just in case *she* talks to you...because...I had told *her*...*what* you did that day.
>
> SHERIFF: Huh?

The idea of telling the sheriff that she had talked with a female colleague about this was likely the monitoring officer's idea, because beginning their conversation in this way would provide the woman a good reason for talking about an issue that seemed more nonconfrontational than the sheriff might believe it really was. In other words, she is saying that there may be some gossip floating around about this and I thought I'd better talk with you first. This could keep the sheriff from uttering immediate denials. Her "this" and "what you did," however, are even more unspecific and ambiguous. The sheriff had certainly made a pass at her, kissed her and, as he admitted, patted her on the rear as she walked away. He could wonder if her "it" and "what you did" referred to these acts, which was likely his own schema. Note also that during this brief conversation the sheriff says "Huh?" twice. It's difficult to determine how much his hearing loss affected his responses throughout their conversation.

TRANSCRIPT INACCURACY

One disagreement between the government's transcript and the defense version is in the following passage where the prosecution inserted the word "in" where it ultimately could not be heard by either side, even after multiple listenings and enhancement:

> W: And then...I had told her, remember when I had a pain in my side?
> S: Uh-huh.
> W: And then you wanted to feel it and then you went down [government transcript adds "in"] my pants and you were feeling (inaudible)...
> S: So what did she have to say?

Other than the prosecution transcript's addition of a nonexistent syllable or word, several things can be said about this exchange. First, the woman was beginning to be more explicit, but not as explicit as the prosecution's transcript indicated. Since she was wearing a pants suit, going "down her pants" to feel where her pain was located also could be understood as his offering her helpful but questionably appropriate assistance. But by adding an "in" that simply was not there, the government transcript made it look inculpatory.

Likewise, her following words, "you were feeling (inaudible)" simply added to the government's schema that he was feeling her up, whereas what he was feeling remained inaudible to both the prosecution and the defense experts. It is at least possible that the sheriff was feeling (thinking, considering) that he should call an ambulance or take her to a doctor. No matter, adding the "in" to "went down *in* my pants" with "feeling (inaudible)" combined to make the sheriff look very guilty.

THINGS UNSAID

The final thing to notice about this exchange is what the sheriff did *not* say in response. Often what is not said can be as important as what is said. For example, he does not say, "Oh my God, you shouldn't have told her this," as a guilty party might be expected to respond. Instead, he says unemotionally, "So what did she have to say?" This response is a bit odd for someone who understood that he had just been accused of improper advances. It is far from clear that they have the same schemas or that they are on the same page.

INTERPERSONAL TRUST

It was agreed that some kind of smooching and touching had gone on between the sheriff and the woman before this accusation was made. It is equally clear that one or both of them should have stopped it before it got out of hand and seriously affected their respective marriages. The sheriff apparently thought he had a nice little thing going with a woman half his age. People who have secrets like this have to trust each other to keep them secret. Bok (1983, 5–14) defines secrets as private and intimate concealments from others. The risk of secrecy is that it has a tendency to spread and to debilitate judgment. Secrecy is a form of promised intimacy, but when that promise is broken, it stops being an intimate secret. The sheriff believed that their previous smooching was an intimate secret between them. He thought they trusted each other. The woman obviously did not feel the same way. One could argue that rather than breaking their intimate secret, she should have cut off their kissing and hugging long before this, perhaps even as it started.

Males are expected to make romantic moves and females are expected to be the arbitrators about when to stop or keep going. Romantic trust is based on this. Older and socially unsophisticated males, like the sheriff, tend to be out of touch with the more recent codes for making, accepting, or rejecting such romantic moves. The culture of romantic moves had simply passed him by, as it does for us all as we age. This is not to say that he was right or anywhere near adept in his aborted efforts at romance. He was an old rural sheriff, used to being in authority, and rough in his manners, and his sense of interpersonal trust was naive to say the least.

EXPECTATIONS

As Wrightsman and Kassin (1993) point out, secrets also have expectations. In police interrogations the target usually knows and expects what the questioner is trying to elicit and therefore can be alert to try to fend off accusations, whether made directly or indirectly. In a confrontation conversation, the taping person is essentially interviewing the target and it is the taper who knows what he or she wants to get out of this "interview," while the target may not. Avoidance strategies used by the target are common in police interviews, because targets can be aware of the suggestibility of the questions put to them. Gudjonsson (1991, 282) points out, "people give answers that to them seem plausible and consistent with the external clues provided, rather than only giving definite answers to questions they clearly remember." If the targets are not suspicious of the questions, the information put to them makes the questions less suggestive that anything may be out of place, especially when they are talking with a person with whom they believe they have an interpersonal trust. The less intelligent they are, the less suspicious they will be. The sheriff was naively unsuspicious.

APOLOGY

Because of their different schemas, the sheriff never knew what hit him. To him, the confrontation interview fitted nicely into his schema that the woman was displeased about his moving too fast in their presumed relationship. He gave the appearance of apologizing about this three times, saying three slightly different versions of "it won't happen again." The conditions for an acceptable apology include

- mutual agreement about the act for which the apology was made;
- apologizer believes he's responsible for the offense;
- person apologized to is the person who was offended;
- the offense is explicitly stated; and
- the apologizer promises not to commit the offense again.

Unless at least the first four of these conditions are met, an apology is not felicitous. The media have recently reported the efforts of many celebrities to offer public apologies for their offensive actions. For example, in September 2006, the Pope gave a speech in which he attempted to apologize for a previous address about which Muslim listeners claimed to be offended: "I am deeply sorry for the reactions in some countries to a few passages in my address which were considered offensive to the sensibility of Muslims." Although the Pope took ownership of the alleged offense and responsibility for it (2), he failed to identify the passages or words that were offensive (4), minimized the offended audience (3), and made no promises or assurances to avoid such in the future (5). This had only the appearance of a real apology.

The sheriff's three statements that the prosecution considered to be his apology were also far from felicitous: "It won't happen again," "I guarantee it will not happen," and "I'll assure you it will not happen again," all of which deal only with condition 5 above. He was silent about the important first four requirements of a felicitous apology. Also note that the sheriff referred to that past offense as "it" in all three statements, not clearly identifying the past offense, but rather, leaving it to be inferred. In short, he was as inexplicit in his referencing as the woman was. But when two people have different schemas of what "it" refers to, both can be fooled into believing they are on the same wavelength when they are not.

At the end of the conversation the woman thanked him, saying, "Thank you for promising me not to do it again," using her own definition of what "it" means as well as her own definition of what an apology is. As she said this she laughed, adding "but I should have talked to you about this." Again, if she had indeed talked about this as they began their dalliance, the problem likely would not have occurred. Instead, we are left with two different definitions of what the sheriff thought he was apologizing about.

One major conflict in this case was that of differing expectations, caused largely by a lack of explicitly stated meaning. Whether or not the woman had encouraged the sheriff to pursue her affection no longer mattered. The police thought that her accusation was now supported with the physical language evidence used in the confrontation meeting.

CONFESSION

If the sheriff did not apologize, did he confess? Wrightsman and Kassin (1993, 6) speak about this same need for explicitness: "What is missing in most accounts of a 'confession' are the specifics—important specifics such as just what was admitted, how it was elicited, and why it was made." Particularly relevant to this case is the citation in Black's Law Dictionary (2004) of John H. Wigmore's definition of a confession: "An acknowledgment, in expressed words, by the accused in a criminal case, of the truth of the guilty fact charged or some essential part of it" The "essential part" cannot be dismissed lightly, because that which a suspect confesses to may differ substantially from what that suspect is charged with. As noted earlier, a speaker who is trying to elicit a confession can manipulate the three aspects of the situation—uncertainty, interpersonal trust, and expectation—to alter the other person's susceptibility to suggestions and elicit agreement to an inculpatory statement that was generously supplied by the person tape recording the conversation.

Rather than being specific about his offense, the sheriff gave evidence of being more concerned about restoring harmony and peace in his office. He is concerned about what the woman told her female officemate, "So what did she have to say?", to which the woman replied, "hopefully she can keep it hush-hush." He then told her, "Just play it cool and if she says any more to you and you say you don't want to testify to it." The woman then asked him if he has told Nancy and Charlene about it. He responded, "No, and I'm not going to tell her anything...I'm not going to say anything to nobody to tell you the truth...I didn't tell a damn soul...I don't want it to get out and you don't either...It would be bad for both of us as far as that goes." Even though the prosecution took these responses as evidence of his trying to hide from a serious sexual misconduct accusation, the participants' schemas about the topic differed. He admitted to "carrying on and carrying on, and I took it the wrong way I think." Again, he did not make explicit what "carrying on" means. His report was that it was playful smooching that he hoped might lead to further gratification for both parties. Her definition, unsupportable from his audible words on the tape, was that he was putting his hand *in* her pants and exposing himself, which constituted the basis for a charge of sexual assault.

It also didn't matter to the prosecutor that after the woman and the sheriff had finished their own conversation on the tape, the following brief exchange between the woman and the monitoring officer showed that they both laughed at the fact that the sheriff "couldn't figure it out." Their two different schemas, the woman's use of ambiguity and her possibly deliberate failure to be explicit, along with the sheriff's own uncertainty, interpersonal trust, and expectations led to her accusation and his arrest.

INTELLIGENCE ANALYSIS

This was not an easy case for the prosecutor. But even though the tape-recorded evidence did not show what he thought it showed, he pursued the indictment anyway. It would have been prudent for him to have used the same linguistic analysis that the defense employed.

[6]

EVEN SENATORS CAN GET IN TROUBLE

One of the three sexual misconduct cases involving written evidence that are discussed in this book (see also chapters 10 and 11) is a case that involved U.S. Senator Robert Packwood. Even though the written evidence in his case was originally spoken as Packwood's daily diary, it was later transcribed by his secretary. As a moderate Republican senator representing Oregon, Packwood was best known from 1968 to 1993 for his support of legalized abortion, his opposition to the nomination of Robert Bork to the Supreme Court, and his vote against the appointment of Clarence Thomas for the same position. He often voted against the Republican Party's issues and was the first Senate Republican to support President Nixon's impeachment. Packwood was a favorite of many environmentalists for his role in enacting the Hells Canyon National Recreation Act and as a staunch advocate of solar energy and recycling. Because of allegations of sexual misconduct, he retired abruptly from the Senate in 1995 after being reelected in 1993.

Packwood's legal problems began in November 1993, shortly after he had narrowly won reelection to a fifth term in the U.S. Senate, when allegations erupted that he had made uninvited sexual advances toward ten female staff members. At first he denied any sexual misconduct, but later admitted that these unwelcome advances were caused by his drinking problems, or at least those advances that he could remember. Subsequently fifteen additional women accused him of the same offensive behavior. Packwood responded that these women were the aggressors in these brief encounters. When the Senate Ethics Committee questioned him about these accusations, he mentioned that he had kept diaries and that this document would show his innocence. These diaries, both tapes and transcripts, eventually became the evidence used against him in his Senate Ethics Committee hearings and in the FBI's investigation into the possible misuse of his office.

Packwood was among many politicians who believed that writing down his daily thoughts, gossip, and activities (he called it his diary) would some day become an important monument that would add dignity to his already distinguished career. Presidents Reagan and George W. H. Bush had done this, so Packwood thought he would do likewise, first tape recording his diary daily, after which he had his secretary type it up. And as in the case of former president Richard Nixon, who simply taped everything as it happened, these daily intimate records made during their time in office ended up biting both of them.

THE BATTLE OVER THE EVIDENCE

In October 1993, soon after the senator revealed the existence of his diaries, the ethics committee subpoenaed them. Many of his colleagues in the Senate questioned whether it was legal and appropriate for them to dig into a person's personal diaries. Perhaps trying to add a bit of support for their position, Packwood's lawyer threatened that the diaries included entries that would expose the sexual activities of at least two other legislators, including one fellow senator's extended affair with a staff member. Packwood tried to repair the immediate negative reaction to his lawyer's threat, saying that he had no intention of blackmailing his colleagues, but this still didn't set well with members of the Senate Ethics Committee; in fact, it only fed their curiosity and indignation. In contrast, the American Civil Liberties Union supported Packwood's claim of privacy, citing the U.S. Supreme Court's finding that Congress cannot use its subpoena power to review material relating to private affairs that go beyond the scope of a particular inquiry. But since Packwood let the cat out of the bag about the existence of his diary, this finding did not apply.

When it became clear that the ethics committee suspected that Packwood might also be guilty of criminal violations, he agreed to surrender 5,000 pages of entries up to 1989. He offered to let counsel look at the remaining 3,200 pages, but not to make copies them. After reviewing these pages, the committee chair, Senator Mitch McConnell, observed that they raised questions about his possible violation of one or more laws, including misuse of campaign donations. When the ethics committee suspects criminality, it is obliged to report this to the Department of Justice (DOJ), and it was shortly after this that the DOJ began to investigate Packwood.

THE SENATE INVESTIGATION'S SLOW PROGRESS

The Senate's investigation proceeded slowly into 1994 and included interviews of various people, the complaining women in particular. The Senate Ethics Committee finally announced that its 264 witnesses and 11 depositions had provided what the committee considered substantial credible evidence supporting ethics violations by the senator, but since he refused to participate in a public hearing about these accusations, this only fanned the fuel for his possible impeachment. Meanwhile, the senator began to try to rehabilitate his standing with fellow Senate Republicans, changing his previous Republican maverick status on such issues as whether employers should pay their workers' health insurance, stating that he had switched his position, and hoping that members of his political party might stand by him in his time of trouble. At almost the same time a federal grand jury began to investigate whether Packwood illegally solicited jobs for his ex-wife from four different lobbyists in exchange for political favors. It was believed that he wanted his ex-wife to get a high-paying job so that he could reduce his alimony payments. The government suspected that evidence or at least hints of this could be found in his diary entries. But whatever these hints were, they never reached the level of verifiable evidence.

The Republicans were in the majority at the time, with the ethics committee chaired by Senator Mitch McConnell of Kentucky. Another fellow Republican, Senator Alan Simpson of Wyoming, warned that those investigating Packwood might not like the results, saying, "What do you think happens in these kinds of situations where you are trying to destroy a person? People get destroyed in the process." After California Democratic Senator Barbara Boxer insisted that the hearings should be open, as were all other hearings that the committee had conducted, Senator McConnell echoed Senator Simpson's warning. Senator McConnell responded to Senator Boxer that if the hearings were opened, he then would call for open hearings on the role of Massachusetts Democratic Senator Edward Kennedy concerning the 1969 Chappaquiddick tragedy, as well as into the allegations against South Dakota Democratic Senator Thomas Daschle's role in an air charter company. Mississippi Republican Senator Trent Lott also joined the fray, saying that one good threat deserves another. Sometimes politics and law make interesting bedfellows.

THE DEPARTMENT OF JUSTICE DECIDES NOT TO INDICT

In June 1995, after an eighteen-month investigation, the DOJ was unable to find adequate evidence in the diaries proving that Packwood had solicited jobs from lobbyists for his ex-wife in exchange for political favors. The text of the DOJ's letter, sent to the senator's attorney, is reproduced here in its entirety:

> This will inform you that the Public Integrity Section has declined to prosecute and closed its investigation of allegations that your client, United States Senator Robert Packwood, arranged for certain individuals to make job offers to his wife in exchange for official acts.

The DOJ's probe, however, did not cover one of the allegations under review by the Senate Ethics Committee—Packwood's possible obstruction of justice by altering his diary evidence in order to eliminate accusations of sexual misconduct. Whenever the ethics committee suspects that a federal law has been violated, Senate rules require them to report this to the DOJ for further investigation. The ethics committee's duty was to consider questions of improper conduct rather than violations of law, but if they discover any possible obstruction of justice during their investigation they have the obligation to report it. So if the ethics committee could find alterations in the diaries, Packwood would not yet be off the legal hook. This narrowed down the linguistic work to be done.

My linguistic analysis of the spoken and written diary evidence was severely handicapped by various restrictions. I was allowed to listen to the tapes and read the diaries, but only in the lawyer's office. I was permitted to take any notes I wanted, but could not make photocopies of anything to take to my office and analyze.

By this time Packwood's attorneys had narrowed down the most important entries that the prosecution might use to about fifty, and these fifty became the focus of my attention.

Once I was authorized to listen to all the tapes that Packwood's attorney had not yet given to the ethics committee and to the federal investigators, it soon became clear to me that his diary was, indeed, just a diary. The senator wrote cathartically, sometimes being mellow, sometimes eloquent, sometimes self-congratulatory, and sometimes self-deprecating. The entries were usually very personal, disjointed, and full of rough language. Clearly he was speaking to himself about anything and everything that happened on a given day. He claimed that he never meant for his diary to be read by anyone and that he never went over the entries and altered or corrected them. It is difficult to imagine why a politician would keep a diary for posterity if he wanted nobody else to read it. But this case was replete with such contradictions.

THE LINGUISTIC WORK

One of the first things I recognized was that legal issues can be overwhelmed by the political process. I had encountered this in 1985, when I analyzed the undercover tape recordings relating to the impeachment hearings of New Jersey Senator Harrison A. Williams. Previously he had been convicted of bribery at trial, but the evidence and arguments used against him were flimsy at best and highly suspicious. However, he was so confident that he would be found innocent that he didn't even bother to hire a criminal attorney, instead using his personal business lawyer to defend him. Nor did he seek the help of a linguist. This was a bad mistake, because the prosecutor ate him up. Now convicted, he faced impeachment, which was his last (and ultimately futile) effort to try to prove his innocence, at least to his Senate colleagues.

I carried out a linguistic analysis of all of the undercover tapes in preparation for his impeachment hearing and showed how they countered the trial jury's decision (Shuy 1993, 20–35). I produced a fifty-page report, replete with charts and analysis to prove my point. I personally gave this report to every senator who was willing to read it. A total of four senators accepted the invitation to sit with me in Williams's office as I went through it with them.

My last effort was to testify before the entire U.S. Senate, where all 100 senators were required to attend. Since Senate rules forbid anyone but senators, the Senate clerk, and the Senate's chaplain to speak aloud on the Senate floor, certain of the relevant and most important excerpts of my report had to be read aloud by the Senate clerk while I stood by, silently pointing to the charts that the clerk referenced. When it came time for questions from the senators, I had to whisper my answers to Senator Williams, whose seat I sat next to, and he voiced my responses for me.

This was one of most bizarre experiences I had ever had in any legal proceedings, and it was one of the more frustrating experiences in my career. If an expert witness's language rights are limited on the witness stand, they are even more so in a proceeding in which the witness is not even allowed to talk. The senators sitting in judgment had a strong schema of Williams's guilt from the outset, largely, I would think, because Williams had already been found guilty at trial. They were not disposed to hear that there was compelling linguistic evidence that his trial result was unjust and inaccurate. It would be political suicide for the senators to tell their constituents that they voted not to impeach a colleague who had been sentenced to three years in prison, whether or not that sentence was justifiable. Politics trumps justice.

Now back to Senator Packwood's case. After three years the Senate Ethics Committee and federal investigators had accumulated many accusations and a great deal of newspaper publicity.

Packwood faced an uphill battle similar to the one that Senator Williams had faced. Eventually Packwood's lawyer and I narrowed down the possibly incriminating evidence that was relevant for linguistic analysis to only the few diary entries that appeared to suggest any possible support to the federal government's potential accusations of criminal behavior. We were prepared to deal with these if it became necessary. One of the most important attributes of linguistic analysis in court cases is to anticipate what one is likely to face. The Senate Ethics Committee's investigation into the senator's sexual misconduct was not our main focus at that time. The criminal investigation naturally took precedence. So my analysis of the diaries focused on whether or not any language evidence could be found in them that would implicate the senator in a crime. At that time the criminal accusations of exchanging favors with lobbyists who might provide a nice job for Packwood's ex-wife had not yet led to an indictment, but the possibility that such criminal evidence existed was still looming. Toward this possibility I decided to examine all mentions and references to lobbyists in the diaries from three perspectives: the speech event itself, the way the senator's use of constructed speech revealed his schema about what he was doing, and the accuracy of the transcript when compared with the tape recordings.

THE SPEECH EVENT

I began by considering the speech event, in this case the genre—the characteristics of diaries in general. Diaries are informal in style and vocabulary, written for the writer, not for an outside audience. For that reason, they are not produced in the usual written register that communicates to outsiders. Diary writers know what they mean and have their own schemas. Their diaries are often abbreviated and less complete, as well as less accurate in their expression of thoughts, than other types of prose writing might be.

Diaries generally exhibit a lack of thematic planning, often relying heavily on an unexpressed context. The writer switches topics rapidly and produces loosely connected syntax and vocabulary. Diaries can also be imaginary, in the sense that the writer discusses things that may not actually have happened even though the writer may wish they had. That is, diarists put down what they think others might or must be thinking and they often omit or distort what was actually said. Writers also often include constructed dialogue for evaluative, interpretive, or dramatic purposes. By definition, therefore, diaries are not completely reliable sources of information. Based on the genre of diaries, I was prepared to testify about these language characteristics if the prosecution should introduce entries from Packwood's diary as though they constituted undisputable factual evidence.

CONSTRUCTED SPEECH

I then analyzed the accuracy of Packwood's entries. One important focus concerned how he described conversations that he had with others. It is commonplace to refer to nonexact but nonetheless quoted speech as "reported speech." This means that such speech allegedly captures the gist of the exchanges while using nonverbatim language. Reported speech is by definition inexact, and it is understood to be unlikely that the cited words were uttered in exactly the form represented, making the conventional reference "reported speech" meaningless, because something "reported" is normally assumed to be exact and accurate. If the prosecution planned to refer to such passages as "reported speech," I was prepared to correct this because such passages simply did not ever purport to be totally accurate accounts.

Much of Packwood's diary contained sentences that allegedly represented his version of what various people said to each other in conversations that took place on a given day. Representation of conversation can be of three types:

- exact and accurate quotations of dialogue,
- paraphrased dialogue (usually accompanied by a preceding "he said..."), or
- constructed dialogue (Tannen 2007, 102–132).

When quotation marks enclose the represented speech or when other indications are given that the speech is alleged to have occurred, conventional wisdom is that such speech actually happened. But from what is known about the human ability to remember accurately the language that occurred, the limits of accurate reporting are approximately seven consecutive words, plus or minus two (Miller 1956), and this limit is in effect immediately after these words were uttered, with a significant decrease in accuracy as time elapses.

For example, Packwood wrote about what others might appear to think about his actions and statements on a given day, such as the following:

> I'd like the ICI to try to raise $100,000 for me. I was absolutely crass...pissed at the mutual funds industry. Anyone who knows me knows that I don't hold out a quid pro quo. This is simply a test to see if they're willing to get back in my good graces.

He elaborated on this topic a few days later:

> The word is out almost, that I can be bought for a $100,000 fund raiser... Cliff Alexander has been indicating that he's quite sure

> for $100,000 you would come around... I said I'm still pissed at them. I said "Bob there may be some other way they can show their penance. I frankly don't need their money."

Constructed dialogue like this cannot be judged as a reliable representation of what either party actually said. It is not recorded speech, the way a tape recorder would have captured it. In fact, it is not even reported speech. Instead, it is the writer's later attempt to remember and reconstruct what was said or perhaps even what the writer imagined or wished had been said. This is illustrated in Packwood's diary account of a meeting with another potential fundraiser:

> You supported me because I was supporting what you wanted. There's not a quid pro quo that you supported me.

This is Packwood's constructed version of a conversation with a lobbyist named Jim Moody. The senator's transcript contained no quotation marks, but it signaled that it was constructed speech by his use of "you." This "you" cannot logically be the reader, for diaries are written for the writer, not some unidentified future reader. Whether this report accurately represents what was actually said to Moody is not knowable. What the diary entry does tell us is that there was likely some conversation between Packwood and Moody. It was somewhat similar but not identical to what Packwood said, and the exchange may have impressed the senator and remained in his mind. He was impressed enough to record whatever it was in whatever way he happened to remember it later.

Since Packwood usually dictated his diary entries many hours after the conversations occurred, sometimes even as many as seven days afterward, the likelihood of exactness in his quotations is minimal to none. Paraphrased dialogue makes no claims for exactness. Reported speech cannot be considered "reported." This leaves it as constructed speech, the term that best described much of the focus of attention in this case.

Constructed speech resembles the dialogue found in fiction writing, in that it is part of the creative act rather than a verbatim representation of reality. In conversation, as in fiction writing, the creation of dialogue has the effect of animating the story being told, making it come alive in ways that mere description does not. For this reason it is commonplace in conversation for speakers to retell an event with "he said... she said" constructed speech. Telling and retelling stories is one of the important means by which we organize and understand the world. Constructed speech heightens the active participation of listeners, involving them in the story (Tannen 2007). The senator did not shy away from involving himself in most of his writing.

Even though constructed speech is more a creative reconstruction than a factual report, most people take constructed speech very literally. They assume that the constructed reporting is accurate and complete, largely because they were not present at the time the words were spoken and have no way to verify their accuracy. Their schema is not only that the writer is reporting accurately, but they also labor under the false belief that communication is no more than the exchange of information in which language is the medium. Linguists know that communication is much more than this, including the representation of values, beliefs, attitudes, and emotions. Therefore, as Tannen (2007) points out, the term "constructed speech" is preferred over "reported speech" because such constructions are creative reconstructions rather than factual reports. It was obvious that Packwood wrote about past real or imagined conversations and later readers could not depend on the entries as representations of an accurate version of reality. I was also prepared to discuss this issue if it were to come up at trial.

ACCURACY OF THE EVIDENCE

One of the tasks of linguistic analysis of evidence is to determine the accuracy of the written transcript. Comparison of Packwood's tapes with his secretary's written transcription was also a factor in this case, albeit not a huge one. She had been doing this task for the senator for twenty-eight years and had grown accustomed to correcting his syntax and making sense out of his obscurities. In my comparison of the tapes with the transcripts, I found that she sometimes changed the tense of his verbs, such as his "we'll" for her "we had," his "we've" for her "we'd," and his "discuss" for her "discussed." She also changed some of his modals, as in her "would" for his "might." She omitted some of his words and phases entirely, such as his "to the federal government," "complaints of," and "I represent." She substituted some of her own words for his, as when his "a person" became her "anybody," his "after" became her "asking," and his "service" became her "system." Occasionally Packwood directed his comments to his secretary, such as "excuse me, I get emotional just talking about it." These asides did not appear in her transcript.

All of this information was communicated to the defense attorney for use if the issue of accuracy were to come up at trial. We were prepared to say that if the transcript changed the senator's oral dictation in matters of verb tense, mood, and noun person, and if it added words that were not there and omitted words that were there, it would be a very unreliable source of information about this actual actions and would be unreliable evidence against him in a criminal case.

INTELLIGENCE ANALYSIS

It turned out that none of these factors played a role in the federal prosecutor's decision to not indict Packwood on criminal charges.

Since the major issue was whether or not the diary entries implicated him in a crime, the prosecutor should be congratulated for his intelligence analysis here. Although Packwood's lawyer was poised to offer a strong defense on specific passages the government might use, the federal prosecutor apparently was thinking along the same lines, and despite the public outrage, he was prudent enough to not even try to construct a criminal case against the senator. The diary evidence simply did not prove one.

THE ETHICS ISSUE CONCLUDED

Even though the criminal investigation ended, the Senate Ethics Committee continued to pursue its case relating to the senator's sexual misconduct—the groping of women. His diary entries, which constituted the focus of my linguistic analysis, had little or no role to play in the ethics hearings because any references the senator made to the women who accused him were vague and imprecise. Eventually he was called to testify before the ethics committee several times, and in 1995, after it became apparent that he was about to be impeached, he resigned his Senate seat.

After a while the ethics committee gave up trying to find smoking guns relating to obstruction of justice in the diaries. It was the testimony of the women he had groped that ultimately ended his long Senate career. His main defense, that he was inebriated at the time of the groping, did not serve him well, and he realized that impeachment and expulsion awaited him if he didn't resign first.

This was a case in which linguistic testimony was prepared for both the criminal charges of the senator's misuse of funds and the ethics committee's charges of sexual misconduct. Neither set of charges ultimately required linguistic testimony, since the government never brought the criminal charges and the ethics committee had such strong and apparently convincing testimony about his sexual misconduct that it didn't even try to use the language evidence found in Packwood's diaries.

Sometimes linguists diligently prepare but never get the chance to present their analyses. This was one of those cases.

SECTION II

Sexual Misconduct of an Adult with a Child

Child sexual abuse, as it is conventionally described, is not the focus of this book. Linguists have assisted in such cases in the past, usually analyzing the interviews of children and suspects by child protection team workers or police. The cases described here do not fall into that category directly. Instead, they take a slightly different twist in which the accusations made by mothers and stepdaughters are based on no physical evidence, on less-than-credible witness testimony, or on confrontation calls that questionably rise to the level of prosecutorial usefulness.

The case discussed in chapter 7 was based on reports of the child's current nightmares that she allegedly reported to her mother, in which the child's uncle appears in her dreams and commits improper sexual touching. Chapter 8 describes a case in which a teenage stepdaughter in a drunken stupor claimed that her stepfather committed sexual acts on her while she was sleeping. In chapter 9 a sixteen-year-old girl accused her stepfather of sexual molestations that allegedly occurred three and four years earlier. The case in chapter 10 involves an adult woman's accusation about her stepfather, who lived in the same house. He claimed to have accidentally climbed into the wrong bed in the middle of the night, but she claimed he did so intentionally in order to fondle her breasts.

[7]

ONE NIGHTMARE LEADS TO ANOTHER

In April 2004 Dora Little, a Nevada mother of a nine-year-old girl named Shawna, accused the girl's uncle, Sam Graybo, of sexually molesting her then five-year-old daughter some four years earlier. Dora said that she had been unaware of this molestation up to that time and discovered it only after her daughter recently had begun having nightmares about it. The mother was now convinced that Sam had actually committed the acts that her daughter dreamed about. Dora reported this to the police, who advised her to try to get Sam to admit it in a confrontation telephone call.

A commonly used technique advised by the police, as noted in other chapters of this book, is the confrontation call, during which the caller tries to get the suspect to admit guilt and apologize for committing the act. Such calls are usually made under the supervision and monitoring of the police. As is often the case, the first call did not provide the needed evidence, so the police asked Dora to make a second call.

SPEECH ACTS: ACCUSATIONS, SCHEMAS AND DENIALS

Dora's first call to Sam was made to his office and it took him totally by surprise. Dora begins by describing Shawna's nightmares and then moves to the accusations.

Call 1

DORA: She's been having nightmares and things and I've been trying to, you know, help her out with it and everything. And she told me that something happened a couple of Halloweens ago with Uncle Sam. I'm going to have to take her to counseling or something if you don't help me out with this.

SAM: Okay.

DORA: Basically what she told me was that, you know, she was sleeping on the couch and everything and that Uncle Sam woke her up by licking her.

SAM: By doing what?

DORA: Licking her private parts.

SAM: (long pause) I thought I could talk to you right now but I can't talk right now about something like that' cause I'm not alone in the office.

DORA: Well you know, can you tell me that's all it was and agree that you'll call me at home or something tonight and just say to her that you're sorry? She said if she just heard you tell her that you were sorry, it was a mistake or something, she would feel better. I'm working hard. I'm a single mom. I can't deal with this anymore, that's why I'm asking for your help. Would you just talk to her and tell her you're sorry? Can you just answer me yes or no? Is that all that happened? Was there something more?

SAM: Dora, nothing. I mean no.

DORA: Nothing more than that, right?

SAM: Nothing at all.

DORA: You know, I'm just asking you for two things. I want to know if that's all that happened and I want to know if you'll just tell her you're sorry, it was a mistake, and let us move on with our lives and be able to sleep at night.

SAM: Dora, I understand that and I will, yes on both accounts.

DORA: On what account do you mean?

SAM: On both, yes to both questions.

DORA: Yes that's all that happened and yes you will tell her you're sorry?

SAM: Yes, I'll tell her that, yes.

DORA: You'll tell her you're sorry?

SAM: Yes.

DORA: And just between you and I, was that all that happened, the licking?

SAM: You can let the entire thing go because nothing happened.

DORA: Well then I need you as a man to tell me as a woman that you didn't have sex with my daughter, that it was just licking her private parts. I just need to hear that from you and then have you tell her you're sorry, it was a mistake, and we can bury this thing under the rug.

SAM: Dora, the answer is yes.

DORA: That's all it was?

SAM: Yes, the answer is yes.

SCHEMA DIFFERENCES

The first things to notice are the different schemas of the two participants. Dora's schema, as revealed by what she said, was that a couple years ago Sam had licked Shawna's private parts and she now wants him to apologize for this. She introduced this by telling Sam about Shawna's nightmares and the anguish this has caused them. Sam's schema, based on what Dora tells him, was that Shawna has had nightmares in which she dreamed that he had licked her private parts. When he said, "nothing at all," he was denying that her dreams were based on reality. He agreed to talk with Shawna and tell her that these were only dreams and that he's sorry that she's having them since they are not real, or as he put it, "nothing happened." When he answered "yes" to her compound question, "you didn't have sex with my daughter?" and "it was just licking her private parts?" he understood this to be related to Shawna's dream and answered, "yes on both accounts," believing that his words, "it was a mistake," indicated that Shawna's dream was a mistake. In contrast, the police may have misunderstood Sam's "yes" as the proper use of the English negative concord rule and therefore thought he had admitted the licking episode, once again showing how different schemas along with ambiguous representations by both parties can lead to different understandings of what was said.

On the surface Sam's responses to Dora's accusation questions, to the police at least, seemed to fluctuate somewhere between nothing happened at all and that he's sorry for licking Shawna's private parts. Closer inspection, however, reveals that Sam agreed to talk to Shawna and tell her that "it" was a mistake and that he was sorry about something, but Dora and Sam held different understandings about what this "it" was and what this "something" was. Dora was persistent though, recycling her topic of challenging over an over again to the point that Sam didn't make his denial as clear as she (and the monitoring police) wanted to hear.

THE NEED FOR A SECOND CALL

With a few exceptions, the police intelligence analysis was pretty good to this point. No doubt they realized the lack of solid language evidence so far and so they prepared Dora to clarify things in a second call. As Sam had promised, he called Dora back that evening, when he was not in his crowded office where others could overhear the sensitive conversation. After the greetings, Dora put Shawna on the phone:

Call 2

SAM: So your mom tells me you're having some bad dreams. I just wanted to say I'm sorry for that. I'm sorry for making you feel scared and I hope knowing that will stop your dreams. I just want to let you know that I really feel bad about your having those dreams. I'm sorry and I hope that helps.

Note that when Sam said "I'm sorry for making you feel scared," his schema was that he was referring to his persona in Shawna's dream, as he clarified in his next exchange with Shawna. Dora heard this, of course, was not satisfied, and broke into the conversation:

DORA: Can you just tell her why you licked her private parts? (*Shawna back on the phone*)

SAM: Okay. Alright, Shawna, I just want to say I'm sorry for the dreams and for you being afraid of me. And I just want you to know that that won't, will never happen, okay? (*Dora back on the phone*)

DORA: But if you'll just explain to her that you're not gonna do what you did to her again.

SAM: Yeah, I explained to her that she didn't need to be afraid, that wouldn't happen and da-da-da.

DORA: Did you tell her specifically why you did what you did? She keeps having nightmares about that. She just wants to know why you did that.

SAM: Okay, put her back on again. (*Shawna back on the phone*)

SAM: Just really specifically sweetie, I'm sorry and you don't have anything to be afraid of, and you know, that night Uncle Sam was drunk and, you know, I didn't mean to scare you or make you afraid, okay? I just hope that everything's safe for you and will continue to be safe for you, okay? Is that alright? I'm really sorry.

(*DORA BACK ON THE PHONE*)

DORA: Can you just tell her that you're not gonna lick her private parts? That's the dream she's having. Please tell her that.

(*SHAWNA BACK ON THE PHONE*)

SAM: Shawna, you don't have to worry about me ever being there at night with you or anything like that, okay? That's never ever gonna happen, okay?

SHAWNA: Okay.

SAM: So I just want you to make sure that you know that you can sleep safe, okay? If I can do anything, let me know, okay? And I know this is rough and I apologize.

(*DORA BACK ON THE PHONE*)

DORA: I still don't understand why you did it.

SAM: I just want her to be safe.

DORA: Me too. I just wish you could tell me why. Why?

SAM: I don't want to get into anything that's going to make this type of situation any worse than it is. I just want to make sure that you guys feel that there's nothing to be afraid of from me.

DORA: I'm concerned, you know. Have you licked other children's private parts. I mean, is this, I don't understand.

SAM: Dora, I have never ever done anything like that.

DORA: Then why did you do it to Shawna? I just need to know, and then I'll let this go.

SAM: I understand, but I've never ever done that.

DORA: So it's just Shawna that you did it to?

SAM: I've never done it to anybody.

DORA: Was Shawna the only one and this is gonna be the end of it?

SAM: Dora, I am not a pedophile. I am not a child molester. I am not any of those things. Please rest assured that I am not.

DORA: This is the only time that this happened, right?

SAM: (sighs) Yes.

DORA: Okay, I would be able to feel better if I know that this is the only time that this has happened.

SAM: I understand exactly.

DORA: Okay. Alright. Well, thank you. Bye.

SAM: Okay Dora, bye.

ACCUSATIONS AND DENIALS

In this call Dora was primed to be more specific in getting Sam to tell Shawna that he was sorry for having licked her private parts. Perhaps trying to explain why his dream persona would frighten Shawna, Sam told her that this dream Sam was drunk. Sam then told Shawna: "I'm sorry for the dreams and for you being afraid of me." This was not good enough, so Dora kept trying, still citing Shawna's dreams, which only strengthened Sam's schema that the only problem was her nightmares. So when Dora said, "I still don't know why you did it," her "it" took on a second stronger but still vague meaning, and when Sam responded, "I just want her to be safe," his reference was consistent with why he just told Shawna that it was only a dream, not with why he allegedly licked her private parts.

Dora was still not satisfied with Sam's responses, so she next downplayed Shawna's dream scenario and moved to a more accusatory stance, saying that she was concerned that Sam had licked other children's private parts, which he vehemently denied. She asked, "then why did you do it to Shawna?" This was Dora's most direct and explicit accusation so far. Sam responded with an explicit denial to her explicit accusation, "I have never done anything like that."

Despite Sam's denial, Dora won't give up, recycling the topic, "It is just Shawna that you did it to?" This direct accusation also failed, when Sam again denied explicitly, "I've never done it to anybody." After a brief interruption, Dora recycled the accusation again. By now, Sam's patience was growing thin and he said, "Dora, I am not a pedophile. I am not a child molester. I am not any of those things." However sympathetic Sam was to Shawna's nightmares, he was beginning to show his impatience with Dora's repeated accusations.

EXASPERATION

To this point Dora had failed in her effort to elicit a clear confession from Sam. But she tried once again anyway, this time asking, "So this is the only time that this happened, right?" Obviously frustrated, Sam heaved a long sigh and said "yes," after which their conversation quickly ended. In both tapes together, Dora had directly or indirectly accused Sam of sexual misconduct with Shawna nineteen times. I charted each of these along with Sam's responses, partially illustrated above. In none of the first eighteen did Sam admit criminal activity or intention. This left Sam's nineteenth response, "yes," as the sole possible indicator of his admission. So why did he say "yes" here?

The police thought Sam confessed out of remorse for his bad act. After all, he admitted that he was drunk and this could explain his strange behavior. But in Sam's schema, saying that he was drunk in Shawna's dream would help explain to her why his dream character did what it did. One major problem the police had to deal with was that Sam showed no signs of remorse here or elsewhere in the two conversations during his eighteen denials of guilt and his willingness to accept that he was somehow a participant in Shawna's bad dreams.

From Sam's perspective, it is likely that he felt that he had successfully denied Dora's eighteen previous accusations and it was hopeless to try to continue to convince her otherwise. At least this would stop her from continuing to accuse him and he could end this uncomfortable and apparently unending conversation with her. It was the epitome of a false confession. Police in their interrogations of suspects have been known to use the same strategy to break down a suspect (Leo 2008).

TRANSCRIPT OMISSION

It is also noteworthy that the government's transcript omitted Sam's long sigh before his potentially fatal "yes" here, but the defense was quick to call it to the attention of the jury, because sighs, like other nonverbal signals, carry their own meaning. In this case, it was clearly a sigh of frustration. Sam simply gave up denying her recycled accusations and vague questions. Like the case of Dr. Desai (chapter 4), there comes a point when people seem to be beating their heads against a wall and the accusation will simply never go away.

Nevertheless, Dora and her police monitor believed that they had finally elicited Sam's admission of guilt when he answered "yes" to this question. No matter that Dora's "it happened" was still ambiguous, because it did not disambiguate Shawna's dream, which Sam had no basis for denying, from his involvement in this or any other any sexual misconduct. Dora's ambiguity was called to the jury's attention, along with the relevance of their consistently different schemas, the speech act structures of accusing, denying, and admitting, and the ambiguity of words like "it" and "that."

[8]

BIG TROUBLE AT A BIRTHDAY PARTY

In the autumn of 2007 the State of New Mexico filed an indictment against Raul Sanchez on three counts of sexual abuse, sexual assault, and sexual conduct with a minor, all felony charges. The event leading up to his indictment was a birthday party for Raul at the home of his ex-wife, Louisa, where friends and relatives, including his fifteen-year-old stepdaughter, Lena, were celebrating. Although Louisa and Raul were no longer living together, Raul had continued in his fatherly role for Lena, monitoring and advising her through her rocky teenage years. They all spent a lot of time together since the divorce, with an on-again off-again relationship.

On his birthday Raul got home from work and went straight to his ex-wife's home, where the drinking had already begun. What happened after that was far from clear, according to the police interviews of Raul, Louisa, friends, relatives, and Lena, who gave highly conflicting reports. The police also thought it a bit odd that Lena did not report this attack until several weeks after it happened. Without the others knowing about it, everyone who was interviewed agreed that Lena had gotten hold of some of the abundantly available liquor and became so drunk that her aunt (or someone else, depending on who recounted the event) had to take her to her room and put her to bed. The witnesses (friends and relatives) also agreed that Lena had been angry with Raul about something, but they were not sure exactly what it was.

Lena couldn't even recall going to bed, but she claimed that after a while she was suddenly awakened by Raul, who had come into her room and tried to molest her. Of course, Raul vehemently denied this, expressing that he would never do that to the stepdaughter he loved and was trying to help grow up to be a respectable young woman.

SCHEMA OF THE POLICE

The police called Raul in for questioning, but the police interview was classically flawed. For one thing, from the very beginning the interviewer was clearly biased in his assumptions, as illustrated by his following statements to Raul:

- "No, she's not lying."
- A 15 year-old girl "isn't going to say something like that if it isn't true."
- "She has no reason to be inventing things."

Because accusers can be as inaccurate as suspects, the police interviewers' first job as they gather factual evidence is to avoid assumptions, including the accuracy or truth in the reports of anyone, including the accuser.

A second job of the police is to represent accurately what the witnesses and suspects said. Based on a tape recording of the police interview with Raul, the following illustrates how far off the mark the police report of the interview with Raul was. Although Raul clearly denied molesting Lena fifteen times during this interview, the police report concluded: "Suspect never denied that he didn't molest her. He only denied that he didn't have diseases." Even this is wrong, because, as the tape recording clearly indicated, Raul actually denied that he had any diseases.

In their evaluation of Raul's integrity, the police overlooked some important things, among them that Raul cooperatively volunteered information that he wasn't even asked about, including that he was an illegal alien, that they could do a medical test on him if they wanted to, and that they should probably talk with Susan and Chrissy, two of Lena's friends who were at the party. Most police interviewers are aware that cooperative efforts are not the typical evasive techniques used by guilty suspects.

When the police interviewed the other witnesses at the party (note that they never followed Raul's suggestion to interview Susan and Chrissy), they got such a wide range of conflicting stories that it was clear that their testimony would neither confirm nor deny Raul's guilt. Those who admittedly liked Raul told the police things that were helpful to him and those who admittedly didn't like Raul told them things that were not favorable. The police interviewed Raul for an hour and thirty minutes, during which time Raul denied his guilt over and over again. With this pile of conflicting testimony, it became clear to the police that another strategy would have to be used. That strategy was, of course, the confrontation telephone call. Under the supervision and monitoring of the police, Lena placed two such calls to Raul.

RAUL'S SCHEMA

Call 1

At the beginning of Lena's first call to Raul at work, he expressed no concern about why Lena was calling him: "Well, talk to me, I'm busy here but, well I'm listening." He then went on to tell Lena, "I know you're unhappy about *what I did* but no, well it's alright honey, but well, too bad. Hopefully everything will work out."

Here we have the first suggestion that his schema of their conversation was very different from Lena's. It was established from interviews with others that on that very evening Raul had forbidden Lena to go out on a date with an older man that Raul did not approve of. His "what I did," in Raul's mind, meant not letting her go on that date. His ambiguous reference, however, encouraged Lena to understand it as molesting her. They were on different wavelengths from the start.

After Lena told him that her mother took her to the Child Protection Service (CPS), Raul asked her, "What did you say over there the day they took you?" She responded, "About *what you did to me* that time when we were at home." Even though her "when we were at home" clarifies nothing, her "what you did to me" sounded ominous to Raul, especially the "to me" part. Now fearing that Lena had possibly reported that he had sexually attacked her, he addressed her "did to me" directly, pointing out the possible consequences: "Well I'll be put in jail. They'll say I molested you. What did you tell the police over there?" She said, "Nothing," so he responded, "Well then there's no problem, tell them that's not true." He appeared to think that Lena didn't tell the CPS that he molested her, which she actually did tell them, but lied to him about it now.

Raul's advice for her to tell them that's not true opened the door for the police to continue following their own schema of guilt, thinking he was telling Lena to lie about his molesting her. In contrast, his advice was consistent with his own schema, meaning that Lena should admit to the police that she made this whole thing up. She appeared to understand this and countered with a request for a directive:

LENA: And so I should tell them that you didn't have sex with me?

RAUL: What else could you tell them?

His response echoed the pattern that some speakers have when they try to deny in such a way that the other person is not offended. Raul often answered a challenge question with a responding question of his own:

> LENA: But what if I have a disease or something?
> RAUL: Why would you have a disease?

To some, asking another question in response to a challenge question is a soft way of denying a challenge when they want to let the challenger save face. There are occasions, however, when a straight, clear denial would have worked much better for Raul, and this was one of them.

INTONATION

His question caused Lena to recognize that she still wasn't eliciting anything inculpatory and, probably coached by the police monitor, Lena then asked Raul two more questions:

> LENA: Did you use a condom?
> RAUL: Lena.
> LENA: Did you use one or not?
> RAUL: Lena.

A speaker's intonation is not conventionally marked on government produced transcripts, but this tape recording clearly indicated that in his answer to both questions Raul spoke Lena's name with stress on the first syllable and falling intonation on the second, a conventional way of indicating disappointment that a person would even ask such a question. This indirect form of denial is used when the speaker considers the accusation naive but without directly and negatively attributing it to the speaker. Instead, it passes off the accusation as unworthy of a well-formed answer that would even require a strong negative form. This type of answer indicates the question is naive and may not even be genuinely Lena's question at all.

Raul's denials of Lena's accusations sometimes also combined the face-saving indirect form with his favorite "answer a question with another question" approach:

LENA: What if it turns out I'm pregnant?

RAUL: Honey, don't be silly. How could you be pregnant?

Whether Raul denied her accusations by asking questions of his own, by saying Lena's name with falling intonation, or by treating them as naively silly, the fact was that even the police realized that call 1 ended with no admission of guilt and no confession from Raul. A true confession requires the confessor to do the following:

- admit to doing a specific act that is considered wrong by specifying what he or she did or by saying yes or no to the specifics offered by the questioner,
- indicate that it was wrong to have done the act,
- plead for forgiveness for the act, and
- include a sincere promise not to do it again.

Since these requirements for a confession were not met, it was clear to the police that a second call would have to be made.

Call 2

The fact that a second call was necessary indicates clearly that in the first call the police did not yet get the admission or confession they wanted. They probably suspected that it is likely that a jury would hear only Raul's exculpation in call 1. This is always a good thing to point out to juries because they often review transcripts of the calls before or as they deliberate.

In the second confrontation call, Lena began by telling Raul,

LENA: They want me to go to a doctor for a checkup.
RAUL: But what will they find wrong with you? Nothing.
LENA: They'll check to see if you had sex with me or not.
RAUL: They won't find anything, Lena. Don't be silly. Why would they find anything?

Raul once again indirectly denied having sex with her, again responding with his own question, "why would they find anything?" suggesting the possibility, to father figure Raul at least, that someone else may have had sex with her. In his police interview he reported that he suspected that she had been having sex with her boyfriend, although she denied it in her own police interview. During his interview, in an effort to convince the police of his innocence, Raul also volunteered to have his own medical checkup if they wanted him to. The police did not follow up on his offer, nor did they ever check out Lena's boyfriend.

REQUESTING DIRECTIVES

It is common in confrontation calls for the police to advise the caller to request directives. This can be useful because sometimes this strategy leads the suspect to blurt out inculpatory information. Following this advice, Lena then began a series of "what do you want me to tell them" questions, to which Raul stayed consistently within his schema about what caused her to be so angry with him that she would accuse him of molesting her:

LENA: What do you want me to tell them?
RAUL: Tell them you made it up because you were mad at me for not letting you go out. Why didn't you tell me you were seeing this guy?

LENA: Because I was scared.

RAUL: Scared of what? When you want to do something, that you want to have a boyfriend or something, just tell me.

LENA: But I didn't think you would let me. I thought you wouldn't let me go out with him because he's older than me.

MOTIVATION

Despite the fact that some twenty times in these two calls Lena accused Raul of molesting her, he never came close to admitting that he had sexual contact with her. Instead, he remained consistent with his schema that Lena lied about him in order to get even with him for not letting her go out with an older man. At the end of call 2 she admitted that she was very angry with Raul, revealing her possible motivation for accusing Raul this way.

The defense capitalized on schema theory, context, Raul's various indirect denials, and the lackof his felicitous speech acts of admission and confession. When Raul urged her to be truthful about his innocence in this case, the police tried to transform his urging her to be honest into urging her to lie. When a jury learns about speech acts, schemas, the importance of intonation, and requests for directives, the picture can become much clearer for them.

INTELLIGENCE ANALYSIS

In addition to the accusations Lena made to the police, the required corroborating evidence was far from convincing, including interviews with the other people at Raul's birthday celebration, the interview with Raul himself, and the two confirmation calls. A prudent prosecutor would have recognized the weakness of his case and dropped the charges before trial. Instead, he plowed ahead with inadequate intelligence gathering and based his case on equally inadequate intelligence analysis.

[9]

REMEMBERING SEXUAL MISCONDUCT

This case grows out of one of those complicated divorce situations that are usually followed by anger and recrimination. Ken Martin and his wife lived in Florida but had divorced several years earlier, after which he relocated in Hawaii. Their daughter, Mary, remained in Florida in her mother's custody until she went to live with her father for a short period when she was sixteen, then she moved back to Florida with her mother again. After she moved back, Ken and Mary argued over the phone about her not returning the keys to his house and some money that she owed him. Several other phone calls followed, and Mary became furious with her father and told her mother that Ken had sexually molested her three years earlier, while she was in upper elementary and middle school, before the divorce. Since Mary's specific memory for reporting to the police about exactly what happened during what time period was weakened by the passage of time, three general time periods became the agreed upon time references: (1) what happened when she was in elementary school, (2) what happened when she was in middle school, and (3) what happened in Hawaii. Mary also used other time markers, relating to the houses they lived in at any given time, but these became hopelessly difficult for even the interviewing officer to keep straight. Specific dates were apparently too difficult for Mary to manage or remember.

Mary's mother was admittedly still very angry with Ken about their divorce, and it is difficult to know whether the accusations made by Mary were instigated the police action or whether they were encouraged, if not invented, by her mother. Whatever the motivation, Mary's mother brought in the police, who first interviewed Mary and then recorded four telephone calls between Ken and Mary. These recorded calls, along with the police interview statement made by one of Mary's close friends during the period (unclear even to the friend whether it was elementary or middle school), served as the evidence to support Mary's accusation.

THE POLICE INTERVIEW WITH MARY

At the outset of the case, the police interviewed Mary. The interviewing officer was less than competent as a fact finder, for she assumed Ken's guilt from the start and often spoon-fed Mary the answers she apparently wanted to hear. As in some other criminal investigations, the policewoman began with a schema of guilt and then probed for facts that would support her own schema. This interview cannot be characterized as a pure fact-finding investigation. For example, the officer begins her questionning with a clear and inappropriate schema of Ken's guilt:

> Officer: I don't want you to have to give me like a half-ass statement, you know. We won't let him get away with it. So unfortunately, I'm gonna have to really dig to be specific so that we can do something to get him taken care of for this, okay? There's nothing you could have done to prevent this. It's not that you wanted it and your mentality was not able to decide if this was right for you. You were brainwashed. Your dad manipulated you. He had you believing this was okay. It's not your fault. What do you want to see happen to him after this?

So from the very start, the result was more like a therapy session than a fact-finding interview of the sort that police are urged and trained to do.

> Forensic interviewing is characterized by skeptical neutrality on the part of the interviewer, techniques that are grounded in research on the development of memory and language, concern about the possibility of interviewer influence, and the collection of data that require minimal interpretation . . . clinicians generally assume that their clients are telling the truth . . . information collected in clinical interviewing often is aided by techniques that lack scientific validation and that require subjective interpretation" (Poole and Lamb 2002 107).

The officer's introductory statements were consistent with the rest of this interview, as the officer continued to lead Mary to provide only convincing evidence against Ken, while believing everything Mary said without challenging any of her accusations, even when they were contradictory.

Although Mary's statements were unchallenged, only partially probed, and even contradictory, to Ken's defense attorney they still gave the appearance of being devastating. A major problem for the prosecution was that in interviews of this type, one does not expect to find inconsistency in the interviewee's statements and responses. For example, at first we heard Mary stating that Ken had rubbed her vagina many times when she was in elementary school: "It would happen maybe once every other day." She claimed that Ken would do oral sex on her and masturbate himself but he would *not* make her do oral sex on him. We also learned that her friend, Barbara, would often be at their house when "he watched and helped them go down on each other." Then shortly after this, referring to the same time period, Mary contradicted herself, claiming that Ken actually *did* make her perform oral sex on him and that he would do the same on her, adding that he did *not* penetrate her vagina with his penis. Still later in the same interview and still referring to the same time period, she added that Ken actually *did* penetrate her during this same elementary school period:

> POLICE: Did he ever at any time actually penetrate you?
> MARY: He tried to.
> POLICE: And did he actually put his penis into your vagina?
> MARY: Yeah.

Two minutes later in the same interview she contradicted herself again, saying:

> MARY: I *don't* think he penetrated me yet but he was, you know, come on top of me and then he would, what is it called, rubbing on top of each other.

Referring again to this same elementary school time period after Ken had moved out and while Mary was living with her mother and she would visit Ken sometimes, Mary observed:

> POLICE: Would he actually ever penetrate you?
> MARY: *Yes.*
> POLICE: How often would it happen?
> MARY: Almost every night.
> POLICE: So up until then he had not penetrated you. He had just rubbed your vaginal area? He had tried to put his penis in you but was unsuccessful?
> MARY: Right.

These statements are obviously inconsistent with what she said earlier, when she said he had not penetrated her vagina while she was still in elementary school. There were other inconsistencies in her testimony as well. Mary couldn't recall many other things that the interviewer asked her, including her former addresses, the names of the apartments they lived in, the year things happened and how old she was at the time, when her parents separated, what the "it" of "it happened" referred to, and whether "it" happened when she was in elementary school or middle school. Her memory was far from good and her statements were far from consistent.

THE CONFRONTATION CALLS

Shortly after Mary made her accusations to the police, her mother told Ken's mother about the charges. Ken's mother, who had considerable animosity toward Ken's ex-wife, then passed the information along to her son, who hired a lawyer who advised him not to speak further with Mary or anyone else about this. But under police supervision, Mary called him anyway, and Ken was foolish enough to talk with her four times, even though he suspected that the calls were being recorded.

In the first two calls, Mary told her father that they had a "problem" that they needed to discuss. Following are the relevant excerpts of these calls:

Call 1

MARY: Why have you been ignoring my phone calls?

KEN: I really can't talk to you but call grandma and she'll tell you why.

MARY: Why can't you talk to me?

KEN: I can't. I really can't.' Cause of what your mother said to my mother.

MARY: No. I want to talk to you.

KEN: Baby, I can't. I'm sorry. Because of what she said.

Call 2

KEN: I can't talk to you because a lawyer told me not to. I don't feel like going to jail for two hundred years because of what your mother's doing. Because of what she said.

MARY: You can't talk to me at all?

KEN: It's how your mother went about it. I had to find a lawyer after what your mother did. She said she was going to the police and I was gonna go to jail. You could have talked to me face to face.

MARY: Bullshit. Don't give me that crap, okay?

KEN: No, you could have talked to me face to face.

MARY: I'm just asking a question to help me, to make me feel better.

KEN: I've been trying to.

MARY: It hasn't helped at all. So I just wanna know why, why do we even have to go through this?

KEN: Go through what, baby? The problems that we have?

These excerpts of the first two calls do not report all the times that Mary asked her father why he won't talk with her (seven times in all), even after he explained to Mary that her mother was the cause of this problem. Most people do not tolerate such constantly repeated topics in a conversation. The fact that Ken did not stop her and say, "Why do you keep saying the same thing?" or "How many times do I have to tell you?" suggests that he had a great deal of tolerance for Mary and that he believed, as he asserted, that the whole issue was the creation of his vindictive ex-wife. After all, he was Mary's father and she was still only a sixteen-year-old girl. Maybe he cut

Mary some slack here. He was on the defensive with a daughter he claimed to love and his clearly reported schema was that this is all a story made up by his angry ex-wife, and so perhaps his tolerance for her repetitiveness was understandable.

Ken and Mary had been having ongoing problems about the money and some keys that she hadn't returned before she moved back with her mother. Ken's use of the present tense in his "the problems that we have" suggests that the money and keys were that ongoing problem that she was so vague about representing. That was Ken's schema. Mary seemed to understand his confusion and tried to clarify, but she was still vague:

MARY: No, the things that we did.
KEN: I can't talk on the phone, and if I'm being recorded, I don't know.
MARY: Whatever. That doesn't, I don't know why…
KEN: Your mother calls up. She upset my mother. She did all this shit. She said all this shit.
MARY: Okay, she upset your mother with the truth? Is that what it is?
KEN: I'll talk to you later.

The topics introduced and recycled by Ken to his stepdaughter were obvious clues to what was on his mind. In these first two calls, his four repeated topics were

- that he can't talk on the phone and would rather speak with her in person about this,
- that their problem was their ongoing argument about the keys and money,
- that he loves her as evidenced by his use of endearing terms, and

- that her mother, his ex-wife, was the cause of the accusation against him.

Ken's topics reveal his conversational agenda and reflect his schema. Perhaps recognizing this, the police had Mary make a third confrontation call.

THE LACK OF SPECIFICITY

In call 3 Mary still wasn't specific as she tried to get Ken to talk about his alleged sexual misconduct.

Call 3

MARY: Well I wanna talk about what happened in the past.
KEN: Anything that happened in the past is not gonna happen anymore, you know, all the fights, anything.
MARY: I'm not talking about the fights. I'm talking about the things that happened between you and me.
KEN: Anything. Anything.
MARY: Like what? You're not being specific.
KEN: Just anything. For one, we're not even gonna live together.
MARY: Who says we're not gonna live together?
KEN: We're not gonna live together when you come back. I want you to know that I'm not ignoring you. That I love you and everything, okay? And that I'd never do anything to hurt you and I'm very sorry.
MARY: So when are you gonna call me back?
KEN: Not right now. I'll talk to you later.

Mary now moved from her vague use of "problem" to an only slightly less vague "what happened in the past" and "things that happened between you and me." Curiously, it was Mary who then accused Ken of not being specific, which was too not surprising since she was trying to elicit an admission and confession from him in his own words. Ken said he was sorry, but this was also vague, for he didn't say what he was sorry for. A felicitous apology requires the apologizer to express his alleged offense. Mary tried to get him to say this, but she failed. She recognized that he was still referring to their fights in the past and so she fished for something more. All he contributed was that they won't be living together if she comes back to Hawaii, which only supported his understanding that Mary was referring to their apparent frequent fights there in the past. Since call 3 still did not provide the police with enough information to indict Ken, they had Mary make yet another call.

Call 4

There was nothing useful for the prosecution in this very brief call 4, in which Ken suggested that Mary email him if she wanted to. He was also surprised to learn that Mary had dropped out of high school and now had a job.

Mary turned out to be a rather inept confrontation caller and the police were left with nothing better to use against him than his "I'm sorry" in call 3. It was all they could get that was even close to being considered an apology for molesting Mary, although still not quite enough to go to court with. They apparently wanted more evidence, so they interviewed Mary's childhood friend, Barbara.

THE INTERVIEW WITH BARBARA

Mary's childhood friend, Barbara, had moved to another city, but after considerable searching the police finally located her and brought her in for questioning. Barbara's exact memory was no better than Mary's as she recalled that she and Mary were in either "maybe fifth, maybe sixth grade, probably like fifth grade" together (following the agreed upon time markers, this refers to the elementary school period). Near the beginning of the interview, the officer asked Barbara:

> POLICE: Who were you involved with? Both of them or just one of them?
>
> BARBARA: Sometimes it would be just me and her and then another time it would probably be like all of us. Like he would probably be like, feel on us, and then, like well if we're experimenting, me and her, then he'll probably like feel on us or something like that.

When the police finally had located Barbara, she was told only that she might be a witness in a sexual misconduct case against Ken and that they needed to verify Mary's accusations. If Barbara was told about the details that Mary had revealed in her statement, it was not evident in her interview. Her information was tentative at first, perhaps being unaware of what she was expected to verify. Barbara's tentative use of "probably" was not specific enough for the officer, so she probed more deeply:

> POLICE: The first time that you remember being sexually involved with Ken, can you tell me what happened?
>
> BARBARA: (*no response*)
>
> POLICE: It didn't have to be directly him being sexually with you but him involved in some sexual activity with you.

Her "no response" here is interesting; the officer's follow-up was even more interesting, because it left open the door to what Barbara had been saying about Ken's directing them in their sexual play with each other. Her words indicated that Barbara understood it this way:

BARBARA: Meaning like directing us to do something?

POLICE: Seeing you guys naked, doing something sexual between the two of you. Have you been doing something sexual?

BARBARA: He would tell us like, try this, like maybe like touching on each other and feeling up on each other as far as like below and above.

POLICE: Would he be naked?

BARBARA: No. He didn't do it. He wasn't taking off his clothes or whatever. But I guess as we started doing it more often he would come in his briefs or like stuff like that or we would have to touch him or stuff like that.

POLICE: When he had you and Mary touch each other, what did he have you guys doing to each other?

BARBARA: Like maybe if we're kissing on each other he would tell us to pull on each other's breasts and stuff. Or like pull on each other's clitoris or there's the time that he told us to try to do sixty-nine between me and her.

POLICE: Did he direct you to get naked?

BARBARA: It was just...

POLICE: expected?

BARBARA: Yeah, basically.

But who expected it? The officer didn't bother to ask. Her set schema was unwavering. To her, Ken's alleged instructions were the same as having sex. But even his alleged instructions didn't take the officer where she apparently wanted it to go:

POLICE: Did he teach you how to perform oral sex on her, or sixty-nine?

BARBARA: No. He was directing us to do this like push on here and then do this and then like rub here.

POLICE: Okay, so he had you put your mouth on her vaginal area and vice versa?

BARBARA: No, but he would eat us also.

Finally, Barbara appeared to catch on to the officer's direction and she began to involve Ken as the director of their sexual experimentation. It would appear that Barbara had a somewhat different memory of Ken's involvement with the two girls than Mary's. It was more about giving them sexual instructions when they were experimenting with each other. The interviewer's questions began to alert Barbara that something bigger was going on here and so she gradually went beyond Ken's directions and added his active participation. Having elicited this much, the officer probed even more deeply:

POLICE: Did he ever penetrate you with his penis?

BARBARA: Let me think, uh. In that, I really should remember it.

POLICE: Were you a virgin when this was happening?

BARBARA: That's what I was talking about. I've been through a situation like this. I don't think so.

POLICE: Did you ever see him penetrate Mary with his penis?

BARBARA: No, but I have seen him jack off.

POLICE: Where was that at?

BARBARA: That was in his room.

Barbara's inability to remember whether Ken had intercourse with her or with Mary is surprising, for that is surely something she might be expected to recall. Perhaps sensing that she should be tabulating Ken's sexual misconduct, Barbara quickly added that she saw him masturbate, but also added that this was in his bedroom. Left unasked and unanswered was whether Barbara invaded the privacy of Ken's bedroom to see him do this or whether it was in the girls' presence. The officer assumed the latter, of course, and probed for more:

POLICE: Did you ever see him put his penis in Mary?
BARBARA: No, I've never seen that, no.
POLICE: Did either of you put his penis in your mouth?
BARBARA: That? No, no. Not that I remember.
POLICE: You don't remember ever performing oral sex on him?
BARBARA: No.
POLICE: So he's having you guys perform sex on each other?
BARBARA: Yes.
POLICE: Would he be masturbating?
BARBARA: Not that I remember. Or he may see us do it and then he may do it.
POLICE: Okay, so when he's having you guys perform oral sex on each other he's masturbating too?
BARBARA: Yes.

Barbara's "yes" to the last question still left open the possibility that she peeked in Ken's bedroom and saw him masturbate. On the whole, however, Barbara's testimony did not do a good job of corroborating Mary's version of the events. Instead, it gave some evidence that Ken saw the girls experimenting with sex and "then" went to his bedroom to masturbate. The interviewer failed to clarify this:

POLICE: Has he ever had you masturbate him?
BARBARA: Not that I remember.
POLICE: Do your remember him having Mary masturbate him?
BARBARA: Not that I remember.

Again, there is little or nothing to corroborate Mary's accusations here either. In fact, they actually counter it. So the interviewer took a different tack, trying to find something to verify Barbara's statements:

POLICE: Did he have anything distinctive about his private area?
BARBARA: Actually I wouldn't remember that. The only thing I remember is him having a hairy chest.
POLICE: Is he circumcised?
BARBARA: No. (*long pause*) Yes he is.

The officer's question obviously was intended to discover whether Barbara had actually seen Ken naked. Since Barbara did not volunteer the jackpot answer about circumcision, which would be helpful proof, the officer suggested it for her. Barbara's immediate response was "no," which she paused to think about, and perhaps now realizing what she was expected to answer, changed her answer to "yes." Barbara's willingness to help the interviewer's schema was becoming more and more transparent. Believing she had now succeeded with the circumcision question, the interviewer tried another one, the use of sex toys:

POLICE: Did he ever use any sex toys on you guys?
BARBARA: Uh, fake penis?
POLICE: Okay, what did he do with the fake penis?
BARBARA: He would tell us to like try to put it in us and stuff.
POLICE: Did he insert the penis inside you?
BARBARA: No. We would always have it. Like we would have it and then he'll be like, try to put it in or whatever and stuff like that. We would do it ourselves. He lubricated it so that it would be more easier to go in.

POLICE: He didn't have anybody do it to you or anybody do it to him?

BARBARA: No.

The addition of the topic of sex toys was also the officer's idea. Mary had never mentioned sex toys in her own statement, but it would probably make a stronger case against Ken if he had given them to the girls. Barbara agreed that they had a fake penis, but she didn't say how they got it. In fact, she said they "would always have it." To add Ken to the event, Barbara returned to her continuing testimony that Ken directed them about how to use it. Again, apparently believing that Barbara's statement about how they used the fake penis would bolster the case against Ken, the interviewer then moved to the standard question about the perpetrator's advice to keep it secret:

POLICE: Did he ever tell you not to tell anybody?

BARBARA: Now that I don't remember. I think it was more so he knew that we wasn't really gonna say anything because we just wouldn't.

This answer was not exactly helpful to the police, because it was entirely Barbara's inference about the topic, not anything factually useful. The interviewer next recycled her earlier topics:

POLICE: When he had you and Mary do this do you know is that the first time that he had ever done anything to Mary?

BARBARA: That's the first time that I thought like, yes.

POLICE: So you thought it was new to Mary too?

BARBARA: Yes.

The officer's "done anything to Mary" implies that he was doing that to them, rather than finding them using the dildo on each other and telling them how to use it. Having milked this topic as far as she could, the officer then recycled the topic of forceful penetration once more, even though Barbara had already denied that this had happened:

POLICE: Did Mary ever expose to you that he had penetrated her with his penis?

BARBARA: No.

POLICE: Did he ever use any type of force to make you do these things?

BARBARA: No.

POLICE: Did you feel like you had to do these things?

BARBARA: We never said we didn't want to do this no more and him saying you have to. I thought it was a new experience for her. I thought it was a new experience for me. So as kids at that age of being curious, it's like we was just curious.

POLICE: So you felt safe being curious with him because he's an adult and that was that?

BARBARA: Basically he was always like, you could talk to him about anything like if it was about a boy or something, he'll always be there to talk to you or give you advice and stuff. I always looked at him like he was just a big kid.

The use of force is important in sexual misconduct cases, so the officer probed for a specific answer and got one that was not helpful about Ken's use of force. Barbara once again denied penetration and that Ken ever forced them to experiment with each other or with him. In fact, she stressed that her sexual experimentation with Mary was a "new experience" for Mary and that Ken's role was more advisory than participatory. It would appear, in fact, that Ken might have caught them doing this sexual experimentation.

INTELLIGENCE ANALYSIS

This was enough for the prosecutor, whose intelligence analysis was more hopeful than useful. All she got from Barbara was that Ken caught them in sexual experimentation and taught them some techniques about how to masturbate. Even this is suspect, however, since Barbara was easily led by the officer's questions and appeared to be trying to figure a way to involve Ken in the matter without lying about it.

At the end, the police had relatively little support for Mary's accusation. The confrontation calls were not conclusive and the interview with Barbara had to be considered disappointing. The appearance of Ken's guilt was strong to them, but the supporting evidence was very weak. The prosecutor's intelligence analysis did not seem to reveal to him the weaknesses in his case, however, and he brought it to trial anyway, perhaps hoping that the appearance of guilt would carry the day. It was a "toss it up and take your chances" kind of prosecution, one that did not bring honor to the idea of justice and one that did not use taxpayer money prudently.

[10]

ON CLIMBING INTO THE WRONG BED

On June 19, 1996, a local police department in Iowa brought Jim Keckoff in for questioning about a sexual misconduct complaint made by his stepdaughter, Sharon. The alleged event took place on June 10 of the same year. The police didn't electronically record their complaint interview with Sharon or their brief follow-up interview with Keckoff in which he strongly denied that he climbed into Sharon's bed intentionally. Therefore they had only her complaint as evidence on which to base sexual misconduct charges against Keckoff. This kind of information obviously would lead to one of those difficult "he said, she said trials."

There is much that can be said about the evanescence of oral language and the relative permanence of the written word (Ong 1982, 123). Tiersma (2010, 17) points out that the legal profession strongly favors the written representation:

> The legal profession has a strong bias in favor of traditional writing...In contrast to the durability of writing, speech is transient. Whatever is said disappears immediately except to the extent that it is preserved in the minds of those who hear it. This is important because people seldom remember the exact words that were spoken.

If the police interviewed Keckoff, there was no remaining record of it. Apparently realizing the need for some kind of report, the police asked Keckoff to produce a written statement describing his view of what happened that night, perhaps hoping that they could find something more incriminating in it. The following is his entire hand-printed statement:

> On Monday night (6-10-96) after 11:30 p.m. I got up from bed to get a drink from downstairs. After getting the drink I went to the bathroom (also downstairs). After some time on the toilet I got up to go lay down. I probably rested my hand on Sharon's her [*sic*] breast. When I get into bed with Traci my hand always ends up on her breast. The next thing I rember [*sic*] is being pushed to the floor and Sharon running up the stairs.

For clarification, Traci is Keckoff's wife, whose adult daughter by a previous marriage, Sharon, slept in a bedroom that was located downstairs in the house. The prosecution considered his brief statement as Keckoff's written confession that he was guilty of illegal sexual misconduct.

INTENTIONALITY

There was no dispute about the fact that Keckoff climbed into Sharon's bed. Instead, the issue was whether or not he did so intentionally. The defense lawyer did not believe that Keckoff's written statement was a confession that he intentionally committed sexual misconduct. It seemed to him that this statement could be better characterized as a description of an accidental event in which Keckoff got confused during the night and somehow found himself in the wrong bedroom. Proving this also would be difficult, however, since it is impossible to delve into a person's mind to determine intentions. So both sides had the difficult task of showing clues to intention.

The tactical advantage in matters involving intention usually goes to the prosecution. Solan (2009, 517) points out that people, especially the police and prosecution, are more likely to attribute intent to those whose bad actions lead to bad results than to people whose bad actions were unintentional. It was agreed by all that feeling his stepdaughter's breast in her own bed was not a good thing for Keckoff to have done. But the police had to show that he intended to do this.

Keckoff's lawyer wanted a scientifically supportable analysis of Keckoff's written statement in order to support his belief that the sexual touching was accidental and unintentional. He asked me to do this in August 1996.

SPEECH ACTS

As I reviewed Keckoff's statement to the police, I believed that a speech act analysis would most effectively reveal any possible clues to his intentions that might assist the jury in determining whether Keckoff was guilty or innocent of the charges. I stress the word "clues" here because there is no way that a linguist can possibly know what was actually going on in Keckoff's mind. It is important to stress this because opposition attorneys often leap on the words "clues to intention" and try to twist them to make it appear that this simply means "intentions." No matter how clearly this distinction is made, the same accusation appears regularly in opposing lawyers' challenges to proposed testimony and, once in a while, even in a judge's decision not to admit it. This distinction is difficult to make clear. I find it interesting that Adam Feltz (2008) and others demonstrate that when a bad act occurs, it is much more common to attribute bad intent to suspects than it is to consider that they may have acted with good intentions. Solan refers to this as a moral judgment that affects our cognitive judgment (Solan 2009). In everyday language we don't normally have to explain our good intentions, but we are usually expected to explain our bad ones. It is apparently difficult for law enforcement and the law itself to consider good intentions that may accompany a bad act.

In Keckoff's case, it seemed to me that explaining speech acts to the jury might assist them in seeing the clues in his statement that would guide their decision about Keckoff's intentions. After giving a brief and simple introduction about what speech acts are, I presented the following chart showing the chunk of Keckoff's language in his written statement, the function of that chunk, and the speech act that it represented.

Language chunk	*Function*	*Speech act*
1. On Monday night (6-19-96)	approximate time	Report fact
2. after 11:30 p.m.	approximate time	report fact
3. I got up from bed	action, location	report fact
4. to get a drink	action, purpose	report fact
5. from downstairs.	location	report fact
6. After getting the drink	fulfill purpose, time	report fact
7. I went to the bathroom	action, location	report fact
8. (also downstairs)	location	report fact
9. After some time on the toilet	approximate time	report fact

10. I got up	action	report fact
11. to go lay down.	purpose	report fact
12. I headed for the couch	fulfill action, purpose	report fact
13. As I was laying down	fulfill purpose	report fact
14. I probably rested my hand on Sharon's breast.	none reported	hypothesis
15. When I get into bed with Traci	habitual action	report fact
16. my hand always ends up on her breast	habitual action	report fact
17. The next thing I rember [*sic*]	approximate time	report fact
18. is being pushed on the floor	passive action	report fact
19. and Sharon running up the stairs	action, location	report fact

This chart makes clear that all but one of Keckoff's speech acts were illocutionary propositional assertions of the facts as he knew them. The lone exception to this is his hypothetical statement (number 14), which reports not a fact, but rather his best estimate that might account for what took place. This is a speech act called conjecturing. Conjecturing is expressed with pragmatic markers such as "possible," "maybe," or "perhaps." In other words, chunk number 14 is Keckoff's hypothesis. In science, a hypothesis is merely the idea that jump-starts a research project that will eventually need to provide empirical evidence to determine and prove the accuracy or inaccuracy of that hypothesis. Relevant and crucial to this case, Keckoff's offer of a hypothesis simply is not the same as his saying it is factual and true.

Keckoff was only trying to provide a possible explanation about why he may have placed his hand on Sharon's breast. I say "may have" because Keckoff's hypothesis, accompanied by his use of the adverb "probably," does not even admit to the possibility that his hand actually ended up on Sharon's breast when the two found themselves in the same bed. However, if it did, this was Keckoff's hypothesis about the way it possibly happened. Contrary to the prosecution's belief, his statement, being only a hypothesis, cannot be taken as an admission that he actually placed his hand on Sharon's breast or, if he did so, that it was an intentional act.

PURPOSE STATEMENTS

A remaining question concerned why Keckoff could report facts with some degree of precision in other statements but not this one. When people narrate past events, they typically describe times, locations, actions, and purposes, but he did not do this in chunk number 14, where his speech act was only a conjecture. Keckoff, like most writers, framed his narration in an action–time sequence, from the beginning to the end of the reported event, with purpose statements interspersed whenever the writer considers them necessary or useful to the reader.

In cases in which time has elapsed since the reported event has happened (nine days in this case), exact time indicators are among the hardest for writers to recall. For this reason people use approximate time indicators, as Keckoff does consistently in chunks 1, 2, 6, 9, and 17.

Action statements are often accompanied by statements about why the action happened, called purpose statements. On some occasions, writers also offer ways to show how the purposes were fulfilled. They don't need to provide these, however, when the purpose or fulfillment is so obvious as to be unnecessary or when they are not discoverable. In his written statement Keckoff has four triadic units including action, purpose of action, and fulfillment, not all of which require a fulfillment statement:

Triad 1
  Chunk 3, action: I got up from bed
  Chunk 4, purpose: to get a drink
  Chunk 6, fulfillment: after getting the drink (indication that he got it)
Triad 2
  Chunk 7, action: I went to the bathroom
  Chunk 7, purpose: not specifically given, likely because to most humans this is obvious
  Chunk 7, fulfillment: not given, likely because to most humans it is obvious
Triad 3
  Chunk 19, action: I got up
  Chunk 11, purpose: to go lay down
  Chunk 11, fulfillment: not given, likely because it is obvious to most humans
Triad 4
  Chunk 14, action (hypothesis): I probably rested my had on Sharon's breast
  Chunk 14, purpose: hypothetical purposes are not discoverable
  Chunk 14, fulfillment: hypothetical fulfillments are not immediately discoverable and therefore not fulfilled

It is perfectly clear that the first three of these examples provide the action and purpose, but fulfillment was unstated because it is obvious. It is equally clear that the fourth triad cannot provide the action, purpose, or fulfillment because it is a conjecture or hypothesis. In something that is merely hypothesized, the action is not verified, there is little need for a purpose statement, and no need at all to indicate fulfillment, since hypotheses are fulfilled only after discovering factual support.

INTELLIGENCE ANALYSIS

This case is about an action and an intention. It is undisputed that Keckoff got into bed with Sharon (the action), although by his account he did so during the night unintentionally and out of confusion about where he was. The prosecutor's intelligence analysis was faulty in this case because whether his accusation is true or not is not discoverable with evidence provided by Keckoff's statement. Sharon, along with the prosecutor, could only infer his intentions, something we can't learn from the evidence in Keckoff's written account. And inferences are not acceptable evidence.

SECTION III

Sexual Misconduct of an Adult with Another Adult

This section reports three very different types of cases of sexual misconduct that were brought by adults against other adults. Chapter 11 deals with a young man charged with sexual assault in a case that fringes on the area that Ehrlich (2007) calls "acquaintance rape" and "simple rape," which is most commonly associated with the practice of dating. In the second case (chapter 12), the defendant was charged with criminal attempted sexual assault and indecent exposure. The third case (chapter 13) describes a relatively common case in which a prominent athlete was accused of soliciting sex from a prostitute.

[11]

A DINNER DATE THAT WENT VERY WRONG

Peter Tiersma (2007, 95) points out that the traditional definition of rape is that the woman does not consent to the intercourse, and that when there is sexual violence, rape is usually the correct interpretation, even when the woman does not actively resist. The best choice the woman can make for her own safety is to avoid resistance, which makes the issue of consent immaterial, leaving the only thing that matters to be whether or not the attacker used force, threat of force, or some other form of coercion. As Tiersma suggests, in such cases the issue becomes whether the man knew or should have known that the woman was an unwilling participant. He offers that the crime of rape should be redefined as

1. the defendant knew or reasonably should have known that the woman did not voluntarily consent to the sex act, or
2. the defendant knew or reasonably should have known that the woman consented to the sexual act only because of threats, intimidation, or fear caused by the defendant (Tiersma 2007, 96).

Susan Ehrlich (2007, 127) describes the important differences between "stranger rape" and "acquaintance rape," noting that law enforcement and the courts have trouble considering acquaintance rape as rape at all. She defines "simple rape" as rape in which a woman is forced to engage in sex with a date or an acquaintance, when no weapon is involved and when there is no overt evidence of physical injury. She points out that if the reported or recorded language used by the participants in such cases is erotic or affectionate, the event is more likely to be considered to be consensual and the prosecution of rape is less likely to be brought as a criminal case.

The first date of David Dawson and Ginny Knapp, college-age students in North Carolina, did not lead to sexual intercourse, but David was charged with sexual assault just the same. As will be discussed, the case had twists and turns that placed it in some rather gray areas. The major task for the defense attorney was to prove that there was reasonable doubt about Ginny's statement that she did not give her consent to their sexual activity after the couple had dinner together. This turned out to be complicated for both sides.

Hormones are good things, but they can easily get young college students into deep trouble—the "sexual spillover effect" noted in chapter 2. This very trouble came to David in the spring of 1997, when it appeared that he let his hormones get the best of him. The unfortunate result for him was that a month after his date with Ginny he was indicted for sexual assault. Perfect agreement about memories of what actually happened in any past event is difficult to come by, and the reported memories of this date by both of the parties varied rather widely.

Here's how it started. David saw Ginny's inviting Internet ad: "looking for a man between 18 and 99." He subsequently communicated daily with a co-ed named Ginny by email and telephone from February to April 1997. They finally got together for a dinner date on May 1. Although they both said that they felt they really knew each other sufficiently, Ginny wisely asked six of her friends to sit at a nearby table, to make sure that David was not "one of those Internet weirdoes," as she put it. After dinner they walked hand in hand to a fountain on campus and talked about the things that young people often talk about—college courses, career goals, marriage plans, places to live, health problems, friends, and even previous sexual activity (she volunteered to David that she was not a virgin). David kissed her on her neck and ear and, to him at least, Ginny seemed to enjoy it. Ginny then invited David to her dorm room to watch a movie. Her roommate, Alice, left the room so that they could be alone. They sat on a mattress on the floor and began to watch a movie. To this point there is agreement in the accounts of both David and Ginny, but what happened next is a cautionary tale for young romance, for males in particular.

GINNY'S ACCOUNT AND SCHEMA

Ginny wrote two statements for the police, the second one coming two days after the first one. When there are two statements separated in time and made by the same person, one can always ask why the second one was deemed necessary. It introduces the same questions raised by the need for follow-up confrontation tapes discussed in several chapters in this book. When the police feel it is necessary to make a second follow-up call, the caller clearly did not gather adequate intelligence in the first call. In the same way, if there is a need for a follow-up written accusation statement, there must not have been adequate intelligence gathered in the first accusation statement. This often means that the defense can be a bit less concerned about the first statement (or confrontation). If the prosecution considered a second statement necessary, the first one must not have been entirely useful to them.

According to Ginny's first written statement to the police, David's kisses "were fine with me," but she reports that she told him that kissing and hugging was as far as she wanted things to go. She claimed that while sitting on her bed (a mattress on the floor) watching a movie, David rolled over on top of her so that she couldn't move. She began crying and told him to stop. He asked her why she was crying and she reported that she just couldn't say anything. She further reported that subsequently he took off his shirt, saying it was too hot in her room and then unbuttoned his pants and asked her to touch him. He then put his hand up her shorts and rubbed her first on the outside of her underwear, then penetrated her vagina with his finger. Then, when Ginny's roommate suddenly returned, Ginny started to cry, and her roommate called the resident assistant, who escorted David out of the dorm.

Two days later in Ginny's second statement to the police she added several details to her first report. Among other things, in her first statement she had reported that he had asked her to rub his private parts. This was now changed to "he forced me to rub his penis on the outside of his pants." She also added that he rubbed her breasts on the outside of her shirt, that she became "hysterical," that he inflicted bruises on her neck, and that she left scratches on his back. Her report of bruises and scratches added the important details of David's alleged forcible behavior. None of this, including the word "forced," was in her first report. It is reasonable to infer that the police suggested that she use more "force" words in her second report, for doing so would improve the accusation of forcible assault.

DAVID'S ACCOUNT AND SCHEMA

David reported that while they were on the mattress watching the movie, he tried to kiss Ginny again. He said that he understood her responsive sighs to be a signal that she was urging him to continue. So they talked and kissed more while holding and touching each other. When he kissed her neck, she, in his words, became "extremely passionate and agitated and possibly upset," a combination of emotions that confused him. But when she then held him and kissed him, he became reassured. After a telephone interruption, Ginny came back to the mattress to lie down beside David again. He claimed that occasionally during the evening one or the other of them would be on top of the other one. He admitted that he undid her bra and kissed her chest, but denied that he ever held her down or used force in any way. He also reported that when he placed Ginny's hand into his pants, she "grabbed hold" of his penis. He also admitted that he first touched her leg and crotch outside her shorts, then moved his hand inside her panties and placed his finger into her vagina. When she told him that this was hurting her, he removed his finger, but she never told him to stop necking, heavy petting, and making out.

When her roommate opened the door, Ginny suddenly jumped up and burst into tears. About this he reports, "Here I was doing what I thought to be an expression of love, with a girl I thought I might possibly love for the rest of my life, and she was in tears because of something I'd done." She ran out of the room and that was the last he saw of her. The resident advisor then escorted him out of the building.

Based on their different memories and accounts of the event, it appears that Ginny's and David's accounts and schemas about what had happened were very different. That night and the following day David tried to phone and email Ginny, but she didn't answer the phone and her email box registered full. Getting no response from her, a week later he wrote her a letter that the police also used as evidence against him. A month later the police charged him with sexual assault.

INTENTIONS

Their two accounts agree about much of their reported actions but differ about the intent of those actions. In many ways they both admit to engaging in rather common, perhaps accelerated, college-age dating practices, where handholding quickly leads to kissing and kissing leads considerably further. Just how much further it leads is normally up to the female to assess and control, because male hormones, once activated, can be more difficult to check. Some might believe that young males are unable to control themselves and that they are after only one thing. There may be a certain amount of truth to that, but the dating ritual for both is often one of testing the waters about how far to go, and it is still largely the female's responsibility to check the progress with clear and explicit language. One could also say that males should do a better job of holding themselves in check, waiting for the female to give them clear signals about how far to go.

But males can be especially poor at understanding what females are trying to communicate to them, especially their nonverbal signals. David claimed that Ginny did not give him any clear signals to stop until her roommate opened the door, and even then Ginny's nonverbal signal of crying hysterically totally mystified him.

Perhaps because the police still had only Ginny's and David's somewhat contradictory statements to go on, and because Ginny was unwilling to communicate with David at all, even to make the confrontation call commonly used in such cases, the prosecutor analyzed the voice mail and letter messages that David left for Ginny in the hours and days following the dorm room incident. The prosecution finally concluded that these messages contained David's admission that he used force, threats, or intimidation in his encounter with Ginny. Based on Ginny's statements, they apparently couldn't justify a claim that their smooching and touching was not consensual, but David's alleged use of force would solidify a charge of sexual assault against him.

SCHEMA ANALYSIS

Miscommunication is common in everyday life. We hear the words of others with our own frame of reference (schema), causing listeners to understand things that speakers may not have intended. We say words that, to us, appear to be perfectly clear but to the listener convey a very different meaning. There are three sources of meaning in any given communication: the sender of the message, the receiver of the message, and the language of the message. It is impossible for outsiders to the communication to determine what the sender intended and what the receiver understood, but the message itself offers linguistic clues to the range of possibilities of those intentions, meanings, and understandings. The issue of what constituted David's schema of intention and what constituted the boundaries of Ginny's schema of consent therefore became relevant to the prosecution and, of course, to the analysis that follows.

TOPIC ANALYSIS

One analytical procedure of discourse analysis is called topic analysis. The topics that a person introduces and recycles are a clue to that person's agenda (Shuy 1982, 1990, 1993, 1998, 2001, 2005, 2011). David's phone messages and letter contain only three consistently recycled topics: (1) he loves Ginny and is sorry that he made her cry, (2) he says he's sorry for misunderstanding her, and (3) he desires to communicate with her further. These topics constitute his entire agenda in these messages. Only his partial attempts to apologize were salient for the prosecution's case, so let's look at those more closely.

DAVID'S ALLEGED APOLOGY

First, it is true, as the prosecution averred, that David seemed to try to apologize, which became a central issue in this case. As noted earlier, the conditions and methods of meeting the requirements of a true apology are

1. there is a mutual understanding and agreement about the act for which the apology is made,
2. the apologizer believes that he or she is responsible for the agreed upon offense,
3. the person to whom he or she apologizes is the person offended,
4. the offense apologized for is explicitly stated, and
5. the apologizer promises not to commit the offense again.

It is clear that David regretted what had happened, but regrets about past offenses do not constitute an acceptable apology, largely because regrets do not meet these requirements of a felicitous apology. David clearly regrets having done something that caused Ginny to be so upset, but he does not know what that something is. He admits being responsible for the events that happened that night, even though responsibility in such cases is usually a two-way street. It is therefore important to determine what David tried to apologize *for* and whether there was any mutual understanding about this. The police believed David's apology was contained in his phone messages and letter, apparently believing that these constituted a felicitous apology. The language evidence indicated otherwise.

Ginny refused to pick up her phone when David tried to call her that night, so he left the following messages on her answering machine to try to make peace with her. His expressions of being sorry and not understanding are emphasized:

11:06 P.M.

Gin, it's David. *I'm sorry. I'm very sorry.* That's what I wanted to tell you. I spoke and I should have known better but *I'm sorry.* And I hope you'll call me at my house, uh, tonight. I'm not, I don't think I'm gonna sleep if you don't.

11:13 P.M.

Ginny, it's David. I know you're not in your room. I can't even drive, uh, not even what I wanna ask you but I'm gonna be sittin' here in (unintelligible) for a while because I can't drive and I'll call you later and if you wanna pick up the phone, pick up the phone. And I hope you will. But *I'm sorry.*

11:27 P.M.

Ginny, it's David. I know you don't care right now but I feel like shit. I hate myself. I feel worse than I've ever felt in my life. I can't drive. I can't talk to you. I'm sittin' in my car 'cause I don't have anything else to do. I, *I'm so sorry,* and I didn't, *I didn't understand and I didn't mean it that way.* And you know that and *I'm sorry.*

11:55 P.M.

Ginny, if you don't wanna talk to me and I'm not gonna bother you. I want you to know that I'm crazy about you. And I want you to understand that I don't mean just tonight. I mean as long as you don't talk to me, that's always gonna hurt. I'm, I'm not gonna bother you. I'll call you later. Pick it up if you're there if you want to. Goodbye.

The following evening David tried to call Ginny again and left another message on her answering machine:

> 7:28 P.M.
> Hi Ginny, it's David. Uh, could you call me or email whatever, uh, whenever you want to talk to a friend like before and we don't have to discuss anything about yesterday. But we can forget it, uh, just tell me how you are and things are goin' and just talk like friends, like before. Please, give me a call. Thanks. Bye.

Now consider again the five requirements of a successful apology noted earlier. Since David is unclear about what went wrong, there is no mutual understanding about the act for which the apology is made (requirement 1). He certainly believes he was responsible for a problem, but he doesn't know what that problem is (requirement 2). It is clear that Ginny is the person he allegedly offended (requirement 3). The offense that David apologized for was far from explicitly stated (requirement 4), largely because he is unclear about what it is. There is no promise or assurance that David will not commit the offense again (requirement 5), largely because he is still unclear about what his offense actually is.

Looking only at felicitous apology condition (3), in his emails David says, "I'm sorry," for the following, again expressing that he does not understand (emphasis added).

1. He is sorry for doing something that made Ginny cry

> Phone message at 11:06 P.M.
> I spoke and I should have *known better*, but I'm sorry.
> Phone message at 11:27 P.M.
> I'm sorry and *I didn't understand and I didn't mean it that way.*

Email at 1:06 A.M.

> I admit right now I'm a fucking idiot. But *I didn't understand. I had no idea* you were going to run out crying until you did.

Letter of May 7

> What happened was my fault, since I was an idiot not to *know better.* When you deal with powerful emotions, you can make mistakes, like I did.

Saying he's "sorry" and "acted like an idiot" does not produce the requirements of a felicitous apology. Even though David didn't understand why Ginny was upset, he accepted blame for causing her to be upset. Notice that still missing here is what the police were looking for—evidence that he used force.

2. He is sorry for misunderstanding Ginny's signals

Phone message at 11:06 P.M.

> I spoke and I should have known better, but *I'm sorry.*

Phone message at 11:27 P.M.

> *I'm sorry* and *I didn't understand* and *I didn't mean it that way.*

Email at 1:06 A.M.

> But *I didn't understand.* I should have known. But I want you to understand that I kissed you and everything else because I was falling in love with you.

Email at 2:55 A.M.

> I realize I was an incredible idiot and we never should have done that so soon. But tonight I just couldn't resist and you didn't make me.

Letter of May 7

> What happened was my fault, since I was an idiot not to know better. When you deal with powerful emotions, you can make mistakes, like I did.

In these "I'm sorry" expressions David admitted that he and Ginny "kissed and everything else." He regretted that "what happened" occurred "so soon," indicating that he admitted that they were moving too fast. However, he did not try to apologize for (or make any reference to) using force, threats, or intimidation. His words were very general and speculative, failing to meet the requirements of a true apology, specifically that there must be a mutual agreement about the offense for which the apology is made. When the sender of a message says and means one thing while the receiver of the message understands this as meaning something different, the result is a misunderstanding. He clearly admitted making a mistake, although he is unclear exactly what this was. His messages also contained expressions of his continuing love for Ginny, his powerful emotions, and his deep desire to communicate with her again, all inconsistent with previously having used force, threats, or intimidation.

David clearly failed to understand what was going on in Ginny's mind. He had no idea why she was upset and he couldn't stand the thought that he did something that made her cry. What David was sorry about was his own failure to understand Ginny's reactions to their mutually admitted lovemaking.

CONSENT AND FORCE

The police had little to support Ginny's claim that she did not consent. She admitted that she encouraged their lovemaking up the point when his finger penetrated her vagina and caused her pain. And they had only Ginny's statements to go on concerning David's alleged use of force. The bruises on her neck could well have been from his admitted kissing her there and she did not deny that she enjoyed this. The scratches she allegedly put on his back were a nonissue, since the police did not arrest him until a month after their dinner date. If the scratches were ever present, they didn't show up then. His progression from kissing to fondling her likewise met no verbal or physical resistance, so he inferred this to be her consent and agreement. Finally, for rape to occur the defendant must have known or should have known that Ginny did not voluntarily consent to their lovemaking. This played an important role in the analysis, for from the testimony of both David and Ginny, such knowledge was not attainable. It appeared, therefore, that Ginny had a sudden change of mind that was not evident up to the point when her roommate entered the room. How David could have understood this was a mystery to him.

This case epitomizes the tragedy of badly taught, badly learned, and badly understood ideas about love, sex, and romance. From early on and from specious sources, most males acquire false information about what turns a woman on, believing, for example, that all women love to have their vagina penetrated as a prelude to sex. From men's magazines young men learn in error that women are attracted to male penises, particularly to their size. Most men, especially young men, are unaware that women consider cuddling and kissing to be sexual, in contrast to the male view that only intercourse meets that definition. Men are usually untutored in how to make "progress" verbally with a woman, bumbling instead in physically clumsy and unproductive ways. But women are not off the hook either. Many expect males to understand their vague hints or read their minds. Often they themselves don't quite know when, how, or where to stop, much less how to make these things clear and explicit to the males in their immediate presence. This common state of affairs can lead to tragedies like this one. And it did.

INTELLIGENCE GATHERING AND ANALYSIS

One can always wonder why the police (the intelligence gatherers) asked Ginny to give them a second report that added information about David's alleged forcible acts that she had not even mentioned in her first report. Was this because the second account now better fitted the requirements of sexual misconduct? And why did the prosecutor wait a month before bringing charges against David? Was it because there never were any scratch marks on David's back and their delay in looking for them would account for their not being able to find any? Whatever the answers, their additional intelligence gathering effort yielded only two conflicting accounts and David's after-the-fact phone messages, emails and letter. That's all that the prosecutor (the intelligence analyst) had to work with as supporting evidence. Unfortunately for him, these messages contained nothing remotely equivalent to David's admission that he had committed a crime or that he apologized for it. Whether or not the prosecutor recognized the weakness of his language evidence, he decided to take his chances and prosecute anyway. He could hardly have been proud of this decision.

[12]

UNINTENDED BUT STILL WANTED SEX

Sexual misconduct is usually thought to be the assault of a male on a female, but this is not always the way it goes. The case of Stephen Ray provides a curious example of the problematic twists and turns of sexual misconduct and its laws.

In February 1997 a criminal complaint was filed in West Virginia against a local businessman named Stephen Ray, who was charged with criminal sexual misconduct, indecent assault, and indecent exposure. As simple as this sounds, things were considerably more complicated. The issues of consent, force, assault, and even the usual understanding of sexual misconduct came into play here. But first, some background.

BACKGROUND CONTEXT

Ray owned a small distributing business that provided bulk candy and vending machines to local businesses such as gas stations and beauty salons. One of his clients was a beauty school in a nearby town, where he first met Brenda, a hair stylist who subsequently accused him of sexually assaulting her. Brenda left the beauty school for unknown but suspicious reasons and started her own struggling beauty parlor business. While Christmas shopping at a local shopping mall, Ray ran into Brenda by chance and suggested that she might want to have one of his machines installed in her new shop. She then gave Ray her phone number to call her and set up a time to discuss this at her beauty parlor. Curiously, she also told him to not let his wife see her phone number because, as she put it, she might think he had a girlfriend on the side. Ray later called the number and set up a time to install the machine.

A few days after this call, Ray delivered a vending machine filled with candy to Brenda's shop, intending to install it. Since he also invests in stocks on the side, he asked Brenda if she had a television set where he could check the stock market while he was installing the machine. Their following descriptions of what happened next varied greatly.

BRENDA'S ACCOUNT AND SCHEMA

In Brenda's account, which was carefully noted in the police complaint and which reads almost identically with the state statute, she reported that Ray:

1. attempted to engage in sexual intercourse with her;
2. used the threat of forceful compulsion that would prevent resistance by a person of reasonable resolution;
3. attempted to engage in deviate sexual intercourse with her;
4. attempted this deviate sexual intercourse with her using forcible compulsion;
5. attempted to engage in penetration, however slight, of her genitals or anus for a purpose other than good faith medical, hygienic, or law enforcement procedures without her consent;
6. attempted this by forcible compulsion;

7. attempted a substantial step towards the commission of aggravated indecent assault;
8. attempted indecent contact or caused her to have indecent contact by forcible compulsion;
9. had indecent contact with her by forcible compulsion;
10. had this indecent contact with her by threat of forcible compulsion that would prevent resistance by a person of reasonable resolution; and
11. exposed his genitals in a place where another person was present.

The police believed that Brenda's account was truthful and accurate. Otherwise they wouldn't have arrested Ray.

RAY'S ACCOUNT AND SCHEMA

Ray's accounts of the events leading up to his arrest were very different.

1. When he met Brenda at the shopping mall, she flirted with him and complained of having no money to buy Christmas presents.
2. While he was installing the candy machine, Brenda told him she was divorced and needed money.
3. When he came to her beauty parlor to install the machine, Brenda suggested that he go upstairs, so that he could watch the stock market news on the television in her living quarters. He went up, checked the market report briefly and was about to come down when Brenda joined him upstairs, her blouse open and revealing her cleavage.
4. Ray told her he had to leave to arrange to prepare Christmas bonuses for his employees. Brenda asked him to give her

"one of those Christmas bonuses." She also expressed worries about her finances and added that she was very attracted to him and felt she could trust him to talk about anything.

5. Brenda then told Ray that she loved sex with multiple partners and that she desires a different man every night.
6. Brenda then kissed Ray while he remained passive, keeping his arms to his sides.
7. Brenda then began to fondle his penis area and told him to open his pants so she could give him oral sex.
8. Ray said he "responded as any red-blooded male would" and let her perform oral sex on him. He testified that he felt "powerless as if I were being raped."
9. After this, Brenda asked him for some money, a little at first, but then she increased her request to a few thousand dollars.
10. Ray said felt sorry for her and offered her $250, the amount of his commission for the next week, but Brenda demanded more.
11. After Ray said no, she threatened to tell his wife about what had just happened. He told her this was blackmail and threatened to go to the police. Brenda responded that if he did this, she would tell the police that he forced her to kiss him and then he took his penis out, began to masturbate, and forced her to give him oral sex.

Shortly after Ray left Brenda's beauty parlor, she notified the police. Since her narrative was all the police had to go on, they knew that it would yield one of those "he said, she said" disputes in court. Therefore they decided to employ the confrontation call technique and subsequently had her telephone Ray in an effort to establish evidence that would support her accusations. This call would be tape-recorded with the help of the police. A few days later the call was placed from Brenda to Ray and was monitored and recorded by an officer.

APOLOGIZING

This call, which lasted three minutes and thirteen seconds, contained the six following presumed apologies that the police thought were sufficient to arrest Ray:

1. BRENDA: I just wanna talk about like what happened last Friday.
   RAY: Yeah, I'm sorry.
2. BRENDA: Why? Why? I mean you pulled your penis out of your pants and...
   RAY: I'm sorry.
3. BRENDA: You know, I kept telling you to stop and you kept pushin' yourself on me.
   RAY: I'm sorry. I'm sorry.
4. BRENDA: I don't know what to do.
   RAY: I'm sorry.
5. BRENDA: I didn't know what the fuck you were doing.
   RAY: I'm sorry
6. BRENDA: I didn't want to touch your penis. I didn't. I didn't.
   RAY: I am sorry.

As far as the police were concerned at this point, things looked pretty damaging for Ray, because to them he seemed to be apologizing profusely for everything Brenda was accusing him of. And that, of course, was their problem. The structure of the speech act of apologizing was central here, since it is the nature of felicitous apologies to contain admissions of wrongdoing. It is important, therefore, to determine whether or not Ray actually apologized for anything and, if he did, exactly what he apologized for. By structure I refer to the required conditions that define the speech act of apologizing. As noted in other cases, the structure of a felicitous apology is as follows:

1. a mutual agreement or understanding about the act for which the apology is made,
2. the apologizer's belief that he or she is responsible for the agreed upon offense,
3. an indication that the person apologized to is the person offended,
4. an explicit statement about the offense apologized for, and
5. the apologizer's promise not to commit the offense again.

Simple offers of regret about past events or offenses do not constitute a felicitous apology. One could say, "I'm sorry that your back hurts," but this cannot be considered an apology as long as the speaker is not the cause of that offense. Such a statement is one of sympathy or regret and does not constitute an apology at all. A recent public "apology" made by a prominent figure was "I'm sorry that this happened." He did not say that he was sorry for committing the specific offense, which could have contributed to a more felicitous apology.

The structure of a felicitous apology provides a convenient yardstick by which to measure the six "I'm sorry" responses made by Ray. The first thing to notice is Brenda's statements to which his six "I'm sorry" responses relate. Features of a felicitous apology are relevant to each of these six statements: schemas about what happened, the meaning of formulaic responses, the lack of specificity about what happened, the meaning of a request for a directive, the difference between regretting and apologizing, and the literal meaning of the words used.

Statement 1

Schemas about the event

To Brenda's "I just wanna talk about what happened last Friday" he said that he was sorry. Since she made no specific reference to what happened, there is no evidence of a mutual understanding about what her "what happened" refers to. It is clear that something happened to make them both feel uncomfortable, but neither party makes it clear what that was. Ray had to infer the meaning based on his own schema. Later listeners to this call, such as the police, and eventually the prosecutor and jury, also had to infer Brenda's meaning. If their schema was that Ray engaged in sexual misconduct, they could infer that Brenda referred to this. If their schema was based on Ray's narrative that Brenda sexually accosted him, they could infer, like Ray, that he was sorry he let her perform oral sex on him. A person's schema is a useful way to extract meaning quickly and without confirmation, but sometimes it can lead down a garden path that results in a misunderstanding.

Statement 2

The meaning of formulaic responses

To Brenda's assertion "you pulled your penis out of your pants," there can be agreement that Ray was sorry that his penis was pulled out, even though exactly who pulled it out was different in their two separate narratives about what happened that day. Notice also that here Ray interrupted Brenda in midsentence and, coupled with his repeated and formulaic and unvarying "I'm sorry" throughout their conversation, it is clear that he is sorry that something of a sexual nature happened during their personal encounter upstairs over Brenda's beauty parlor.

Relating to who did the pulling, in the obviously stressful circumstances of this call, Ray simply may not have paid attention to the pronoun reference indicated by Brenda's identification of Ray as the one who pulled it out. Alternatively, of course, he may have pulled it out himself, having been tempted, as he put it, as "any red-blooded male would be." Their two conflicting narratives agree that oral sex occurred, no matter who extracted his penis from his pants. But the answer to the question about who did the extracting remains as unclear as what Ray was sorry about.

Statement 3

Lack of specificity about what happened

To Brenda's "I kept telling you to stop and you kept pushin' yourself on me," Ray again offered his bare and formulaic "I'm sorry," which by now could not be clearly taken as his either agreeing or disagreeing that she told him to stop or that he kept pushing himself on her. To accept his "I'm sorry" as an admission of his pushing himself on her can be made only by inferring as much. It remains unclear what the specific offense was because, following Ray's narrative schema, he was sorry that he let himself get into the situation of allowing her to perform oral sex on him.

Statement 4

The meaning of a request for a directive

Ray's repeated "I'm sorry" response to Brenda's "I don't know what to do" did not relate to any specific action posited here by Brenda. It is common in confrontation calls such as this for the caller to appear stressed and to ask the target what she should do next. This is a common scripting strategy that sometimes elicits inculpatory responses. On the other hand, if we believe Ray's narrative, he thinks she was inviting him to offer her money to keep quiet so she won't tell his wife about it. In other words, he could think she was attempting to blackmail him, which is what he reported to police when they initially questioned him. In addition, if taken literally, Ray's "I'm sorry" here indicated that he was sorry that she didn't know what to do. This meaning, however, is unlikely if Ray believed she was after blackmail money, suggesting once again that he was in some kind of shock in which the best he could do was to utter his vague "I'm sorry" responses.

Statement 5

The difference between regretting and apologizing

Ray's "I'm sorry" also fails as an apology in response to Brenda's "I didn't know what the fuck you were doing." To be considered one, we would have to believe that he was sorry for not letting her know what he was doing; this understanding would not bolster a case that he did what he did intentionally. It is clear that here he was simply continuing his formulaic, nonspecific expression of regret that the whole thing happened at all.

Statement 6

Problems with the literal meaning of words

Ray continues his "I'm sorry" routine to Brenda's "I didn't want to touch your penis." Notice here that Brenda did not say that she actually did touch his penis; only that she did not want to, which, of course, would support evidence of her nonconsent. Whether such touching ever occurred cannot be retrieved from her statement here, although it is likely that the touching did occur. Taken literally, Ray's response means that he was sorry that she did not want to touch it or, stated positively, that he wished that she had wanted to do so. As Solan and Tiersma (2005, 216) point out, "while a literal truth... may seem appealing, the question of what is 'literally' true is, in reality, highly problematic." At any rate, his response to Brenda's statement, "I'm sorry," did not meet the conditions of a felicitous apology. That is, it did not contain enough specificity to mean "I'm sorry that I forced you to touch my penis." In fact, even her own words don't provide this meaning.

VAGUE AND AMBIGUOUS REFERENCES

Further failed efforts to establish the specific meaning of what Ray was thought to apologize for can be found in Brenda's vague and ambiguous references throughout the brief conversation—"what," "that," "this," and "it," as the following indicate:

> *what* happened last Friday
> why you did *that*
> I've been a nervous wreck over *this*
> I have to think about *this* (four times)
> You shoulda thought about *that*
> Larry (her ex-husband) destroyed our family over *this*
> *It* was wrong (two times)
> while you were doing *that*

As seen in other cases in this book, it behooves callers in a confrontation call to be specific about the alleged offense for which the targets are expected to confess. It equally behooves suspects to be specific about what they are apologizing about. If at least one of the two participants does not make these clear, there is no way to judge a meeting of their minds. Without such specificity, alleged agreements and apologies cannot be considered felicitous.

Taking the law enforcement perspective for a moment, there is an obvious danger for the caller to be specific, especially when the apology seeker suspects that the request for an apology would be denied if it were couched in explicit terms. That danger was borne out in this case, because, interestingly, to the one and only instance in which Brenda approached some degree of specificity, Ray categorically gave a denial:

BRENDA: You tried to rip my clothes off.
RAY: No I didn't, Brenda!
BRENDA: Oh, come on! You tried to unzip my pants and...
RAY: Listen to me. Can I come and talk to you?

Ray clearly denied Brenda's complaint and Brenda then denied his denial, but this is still less than useful for the prosecution in terms of its evidential value. He then deflected her denial of his denial by ending this exchange with a plea to get together to discuss this matter more fully. His "listen to me" is an indication that he believed she has not heard or understood his references when he said "I'm sorry" those six times.

Perhaps unfortunately for Ray, he also admitted that he made a mistake, as follows:

RAY: Can I come and talk to you?
BRENDA: No. I'm afraid. I'm afraid.
RAY: Listen. Listen. Listen. Listen. *I know I made a mistake.*

Yes, Ray admitted that he made a mistake, but it remains unclear exactly what that mistake was. Brenda's version was that he committed sexual misconduct. Ray's version was that he let her give him oral sex but later realized that this was a mistake that could be damaging to his marriage, adding:

RAY: I can't lose my family over *it*.

Ray's ambiguous "over it" was equally susceptible to two different interpretations: that he instigated it intentionally or that he succumbed to her efforts to do it without his objection. Possibly realizing this ambiguity, Brenda continued:

BRENDA: Why didn't you stop when I told you to?
RAY: I don't know. I don't know.

His "I don't know" response to her question about why he didn't stop when she told him to was perhaps his most damaging statement, because this answer acknowledged that she actually told him to stop but he didn't do so. The overall context of this conversation, however, offers some help to Ray's defense. Clearly he was highly stressed, and twice he said that he feared that he'd lose his family over this. At one point he even swore he would kill himself. Under such circumstances his "I don't know" could be inferred to mean, "I don't know what to do" rather than "I don't know why I didn't stop." It is also unclear what Brenda meant by "why didn't you stop." Ray admitted that he let her perform oral sex on him. She may have given him the opportunity to stop her ("when I told you to"), but his testimony that he did so because it was "what any red-blooded man would do" wouldn't let him make himself stop. When confronted in this way, it is natural for targets to think and talk in ways that are less than clear. And Ray was no exception.

The taped conversation evidence did not present convincing evidence that would support Brenda's accusations. There was no dispute, however, that at a minimum, oral sex took place. For some, this would be enough to convict Ray, possibly because he should have called on his moral reserve to refuse Brenda's advance, but that probably would be a moral decision, not a legally based one. As for Ray's account of the whole event, some also would discount Ray's claim that any red-blooded male would accept a woman's offer of oral sex.

INTELLIGENCE GATHERING AND ANALYSIS

It remains unclear from the evidence what Ray was sorry about and what they both referred to when they used the ambiguous words "what," "that," "this," and "it." The police, the prosecution, and the jury could only make inferences about these vague references. Inferences are always tricky, if not deceptive. The linguists job is to point out the words and phrases that are vague or ambiguous, not to tell the jury what they actually meant to the participants, for that would be going beyond what linguists can or should do. In contrast, the prosecutors have the right to infer meanings if they feel comfortable doing so. Or they can conclude that they can't decide issues that are expressed with ambiguity and vagueness. One should hope for the latter.

In preparation for a trial, the intelligence gathering was poor in this case. Brenda might have been prepared by the police to be more explicit about what the alleged crime actually was. The closest she comes to being explicit is when she claimed that Ray tried to tear her clothes off, which he then emphatically denied. One can only wonder why the police didn't see the problems in the confrontation call and have Brenda call him again, using more explicit language that, if truthful, would be more likely to provide strong evidence for a conviction. The fact that they didn't do this suggests either that the investigation was flawed or that the police and prosecutor really didn't believe Brenda's account in the first place and knew that they would have to go to court with whatever faulty evidence they had. It could be one of those cases in which, from the prosecution's perspective, less information is better than more. The prosecutor is not off the hook for this. He should have recognized the problematic nature of the evidence before he took it to trial.

[13]

A PROSTITUTION STING OPERATION

At 3:15 a.m. in Las Vegas, Nevada, on a mid-January 1985 evening, an Olympic athlete had an argument with his wife and decided to drive to a disco to be with somebody else for the evening. On his way there, he stopped for a traffic light at the intersection of Genson Avenue and Sumner Boulevard. An attractive woman standing alone on the corner smiled at him, and he reported that when he stopped, he nodded in response. The woman turned out to be a plainclothes undercover vice squad officer, who was posing as a decoy to catch perpetrators in prostitution. The athlete was subsequently arrested, handcuffed, and charged with soliciting prostitution.

The policewoman's account of their conversation differed remarkably from the athlete's, and these differences framed the case that followed. The officer was wearing a microphone hidden on her purse strap, transmitting her conversation with the athlete to other officers in a nearby police car, who preserved it on tape. The quality of this recording was far from clear, but the female decoy officer maintained that the tape of their conversation accurately conveyed what was said.

The charge against the athlete was only a misdemeanor, usually subject to a fine of less that $1,000, but it had more serious implications for him because it could blemish his worldwide reputation.

He denied that he solicited prostitution and hired a lawyer to dispute the charge at trial. Knowing that the tape-recorded evidence would play a significant role in the trial, the lawyer retained me to determine what was on the tape and to compare the prosecutor's evidence.

THE POLICE REPORT

The police officer's report said the following:

> Officer Sanchez looked at defendant, who nodded his head upon making eye contact with her. The officer smiled at defendant and the officer continued pacing back and forth at her location momentarily turning her back on and losing sight of the defendant.
>
> Approximately 10 to 15 seconds later the officer heard a voice coming from the defendant's vehicle stating something to the effect of "nice night." The officer turned back toward the defendant's vehicle, observing no other persons on the street or in the vicinity of the defendant's vehicle. The officer observed the defendant to still be looking at her and stated to the defendant, "are you talking to me?" The defendant replied, "I said it's a nice night." The officer responded, "Oh, yeah" and continued pacing on the southwest corner. The defendant then stated something unintelligible to the officer, which included the word "gorgeous."
>
> The officer then stated, "I can't hear you, if you want to talk to me, you'll have to pull over." The defendant then backed up and parked his vehicle at the east curb. After parking his vehicle the defendant waved to the officer with his left arm in a beckoning manner.

The officer then walked across Genson Avenue in front of the defendant's vehicle, noting defendant's license plate and informing officer Rudolph, who was electronically monitoring the officer's conversation and her report of the license number and vehicle description as she walked past the defendant's vehicle and approached the defendant's front passenger window, which was rolled approximately halfway down.

At that time the conversation recorded when the defendant's arrest report took place was transcribed.

THE TAPE RECORDING AND TRANSCRIPT

The prosecution's transcription of the six turns of talk that represented the pertinent part of the electronically recorded conversation was as follows:

Prosecution transcript

1. Defendant: Hi, how are you?
2. Officer: Fine, and you?
3. Defendant: How much for an hour?
4. Officer: What do you want?
5. Defendant: Oh, some head and a little fuckie for one hundred dollars.
6. Officer: Sure. Make a right and I'll meet you.

Careful listening to the scratchy-sounding tape recording many times with good equipment revealed what was actually said in those six turns (emphasis of differences added):

Defense transcript

1. Defendant: Hi, how *you doin'*?
2. Officer: Fine, and you?
3. Defendant: *Wanna dance* for an hour?
4. Officer: What do you want?
5. Defendant: Oh *sure, have a little fun for about* an hour.
6. Officer: Sure. Make a right and I'll meet you.

PHONETICALLY INFLUENCED SCHEMA

Obviously the prosecution and the defense heard the athlete saying very different things. How could this happen? One possibility is that the officer's voice, picked up by the microphone on her purse strap, is relatively clear, but the track star's voice, a considerable distance from her mike, is far less audible. Note that in the brief passage transcribed above, there was no dispute about what the officer said. The only conflict stemmed from the words of the athlete. His distance from the officer's recording equipment was a possible factor, because he was in the driver's seat of his car (not a convertible) and the officer was standing or pacing on a street corner to his right. The police report said that his passenger side window was rolled halfway down and it estimated that he was some twenty feet away from the officer as they talked.

The recording had such bad scratchy quality that the transcribers appeared to guess at what the athlete was saying. Guessing, however, is not the proper job of a transcriber. It is standard, ethical practice to transcribe speech only when the transcribers are confident about the accuracy of the words they hear. When there is a question about audibility, the standard practice is to identify the unclear word, phrase, or passage with the word "inaudible" in parentheses.

I have run into the problem of faulty transcriptions many times over the years. Sometimes transcription errors are not critically important, but often they can completely change the evidence in a case. In a Nevada case several years ago, for example, two county brothel commissioners were sitting at a table in a noisy café with a woman who pulled out $5,000 and offered it to them as a bribe to help her get a brothel license (Shuy 1993, 35–42). The men were dumbfounded and one of them said to the other: "No, I wouldn't take a bribe, would you?" The tape was scratchy and unclear while loud, dish-clattering noises and other conversations in the café interfered as well. The police transcription of this sentence was "No, I would take a bribe, wouldn't you?" This, of course, was the keystone of their indictment for bribery.

My task was to help the jury understand this sentence accurately. My superior equipment, training in phonetics, and years of experience listening to tapes as badly recorded as this one would be not enough to convince them. I believed that I needed to find a way for the jury to hear the important difference for themselves. I decided that the best way was to get the jury to listen for the brief pause that occurred and to count the number of syllabic beats on each side of that pause as I played that passage several times for them:

Prosecution transcript

I	would	take	a	bribe, [**pause**]	would	n't	you?
1	2	3	4	5	6	7	8

Defense transcript

I	would	n't	take	a	bribe [**pause**]	would	you?
1	2	3	4	5	6	7	8

I also pointed out that the police transcript had transported the negative "n't" morpheme from the first "would" to the second "would" in that sentence, possibly because this movement would fit better with the transcriber's apparent schema of guilt. The more the jury listened, the more they were convinced about exactly where the brief pause actually occurred.

This approach also seemed to be a good way to deal with the case of the famous athlete. Let's take the six turns in pairs.

Turns 1 and 2

How could the police transcribers guess that his "Hi, how you doin'? was "Hi, how are you?" Perhaps realizing that greeting routines are not that important, they probably simply normalized the athlete's expression to the greeting routine that they would normally say and hear. To do this, however, they had to add one more syllable to what the athlete said:

Prosecution transcript

Hi,	how	are	you?
1	2	3	4

Defense transcript

Hi,	how	you	do	in'?
1	2	3	4	5

Likewise, in turns 3 and 4 the transcriber converted the athlete's "Wanna dance for an hour?" into "How much for an hour"? I told the jury that one of the first things to do when difficult-to-hear tapes are in evidence is to notice the number of syllables. Virtually anyone can count the beats they hear in sentences. If the transcribers had listened only for the number of syllables, they would have noticed that their transcript omitted one syllable that was recorded on the tape in the third and fourth turns:

Police transcript

How	much	for	an	ho	ur?
1	2	3	4	5	6

Defense transcript

Wan	na	dance	for	an	ho	ur?
1	2	3	4	5	6	7

And in the fifth and sixth turns, how could the transcribers guess that his "Oh sure, have a little fun for about an hour" was "Oh some head and a little fuckie for one hundred dollars"? This time the police transcript added six syllables that simply were not audible.

Police transcript

Oh	sure,	have	some	head	and	a	lit	tle	fuck	ie	for	one	hun	dred	dol	lars
1	2	3	4	5	6	7	8	9	10	11	12	13	14	15	16	17

Defense transcript

Oh	sure	have	a	lit	tle	fun	for	an	ho	ur
1	2	3	3	5	6	7	8	9	10	11

So how could this mess happen? One strong possibility, in addition to the distance from the mike and a recording with a scratchy quality, is that the schema of the police leads them to believe that anyone who talks with a hooker on the street wants only one thing—sex. In their minds, any man who stops at a traffic light and responds to a woman standing on a street corner must know that she is a hooker and therefore is negotiating a price.

To accommodate this schema, the transcribers had to stretch their imaginations of the actual speech sounds to a great extent. They had to ignore the number of syllable beats. They also had to ignore the clear nasal /n/ consonant and the nasal /æ/ vowel in his "wanna dance" in order to hear it as "how much." This was quite a stretch, even for transcribers with a schema of guilt.

Another schema-induced stretch of imagination was to transcribe his "oh sure, have some fun for about an hour" as "oh sure, have some head and a little fuckie for one hundred dollars." This increase of his 11 clearly audible syllables into 17 syllables took some heavy phonetic imagination. They managed to hear his "oh," "and," and "a little" correctly, but nothing else. They transcribed his "fun for" as "fuckie for," even though there was not a trace of a voiceless back consonant /k/ on the tape. Similarly, somehow they transcribed "about an hour" as "one hundred dollars," perhaps the most egregious and erroneous transcription of all. One is led to believe that they were hearing what they wanted to hear based on their schema of what they expected to hear in such a sting operation.

At trial, the officer added that the athlete had called her "gorgeous." The athlete admitted that he had used the word "gorgeous," but not in the context noted by the officer. His claim was that he said "gorgeous night," which is very different from allegedly complementing the woman's appearance. This phrase could not be heard on the tape, so this dispute could not be verified by either side. The prosecutor had to take the officer's word about what was actually said. In this case, taking the officer's word became iffy at best.

NONVERBAL COMMUNICATION AND INFERENCES

Three other inferences by the police also played a big role in this case. In her report the officer stated that she first made "eye contact" with the subject and that he "nodded his head" inside the car. In the wee hours of the morning, even on a well-lighted street corner, her ability to see a driver make eye contact while he is seated on the opposite side from her in his car is hard to imagine. She also testified that the suspect was "still looking at her" after she turned her back for ten to fifteen seconds. One can only wonder how she could see him looking at her while her back was turned.

The undercover policewoman also stated in her report that the athlete waved at her with his left hand "in a beckoning manner." Just exactly what a beckoning manner means can be debated. Beckoning is usually accomplished with the fingers, either cupped with a motion toward oneself or with the forefinger. Since she also reported that the window on the passenger's side was rolled halfway down as she faced his vehicle, this would mean that in order to beckon to her the athlete would have had to lean from his driver's seat across the passenger side of his front seat and use his more distant left hand to wave at her in order to make this waving gesture with the passenger window rolled halfway down, a feat that seems physically impossible, even for a world-class athlete.

Another dispute was whether the athlete parked his car the way the police report indicated. The report said that he parked at the intersection after their conversation. The athlete said that after their brief exchange while he was stopped at the traffic light, he drove slowly ahead to the intersection and turned right onto Sumner Boulevard, at which point a police car with red lights flashing pulled him over and arrested him. Yes, he said he stopped at the traffic light, but he did not pull over to the curb at that time and did not do so until the police car pulled him over and he turned right into the next block. In fact, by turning right he was driving away from the corner where the policewoman was standing and toward the disco he planned to visit.

INTELLIGENCE GATHERING AND ANALYSIS

The major evidence for the prosecution in this case was the electronically recorded conversation. The major evidence for the defense was that the explanation of the schema of the police steered them to a creative and inaccurate transcription of the recoded conversation along with nonverbal communication that showed, in the end, that the athlete was not guilty of the charges brought against him. Both the evidence gathering and analysis were far from acceptable in this case.

SECTION IV

Prosecution and Defense Tools

As in other criminal cases, prosecutions of sexual misconduct require more conclusive evidence than a mere accusation, because the complainant's reports could be as subjective and erroneous as those of the suspects. In order to make a successful case against alleged suspects, law enforcement needs to have corroborating evidence so that the accusations will stand up. In most sexual misconduct cases, such corroborating evidence includes police interviews of the complainants and any witnesses to the alleged crimes. These are sometimes accompanied by what has come to be known as the confrontation call or the confrontation meeting, during which the complainant talks with the suspect and tries to get him or her to admit past behavior. In some cases, similar to undercover sting operations, the police make an effort to capture the crime while it is happening by electronically recording the event on either audiotape or videotape.

On the defense side, attorneys have the opportunity to challenge the accuracy of the police interviews and the alleged information that emerges from staged confrontations or any other evidence. In the rare instances when the sexual misconduct event itself is recorded, the defense also has the opportunity to challenge the electronic quality of the recording, the accuracy of any transcripts made for the jury, as well as the specificity and clarity of the language used by both parties.

Chapter 14 summarizes the major problems that law enforcement officers experienced in these case examples while they gathered intelligence as well as the problems experienced by prosecutors as they analyzed this intelligence.

Chapter 15 reprises the way linguistic tools were used by the defense attorneys as they tried to counter the sexual misconduct charges. It also stresses the need for prosecutors, defense attorneys, and linguists to consider larger units of language before they focus on smaller language units, primarily because these larger language units, such as the speech event, schemas, agendas, and speech acts, often can help provide the actual meaning of the smaller units, such as the individual words and phrases that, on the surface, appear to be smoking guns.

[14]

PROSECUTORIAL PROBLEMS IN GATHERING AND ANALYZING THE EVIDENCE

Like all criminal and civil law events, sexual misconduct cases make use of tools and strategies of various types. Prosecutors show their hand first in the form of an indictment along with the evidence that purportedly supports it. After the usual series of briefs by both sides, the defense attorney gets his or her turn to either plead guilty and take the best plea agreement possible or to fight the charges at trial. Often this fight is over the way the evidence was gathered and whether it really says what the prosecution claims it says.

In the cases described in this book, there are many problems both with the way the evidence was collected and the way the prosecution analyzed it. After the victims make their sexual misconduct accusations, law enforcement officers usually produce a written report of the complainants' accusations and accounts, then collect more evidence in the form of interviews with witnesses and suspects, often including a tape and transcript of any tape-recorded interviews. The police often then produce more written reports summarizing those interviews.

In seven of the cases described in this book additional evidence-gathering steps were added. The police had accusers make the confrontation telephone calls described in chapters 4 (Dr. Desai),

7 (Sam Graybo), 8 (Raul Sanchez), 9 (Ken Martin), and 12 (Stephen Ray).

Sexual misconduct, like many language crimes, is difficult to capture as it is happening, but chapters 3 (Dr. Berger) and 5 (Sheriff Williams) describe confrontation meetings in which the police asked the accusers to record face-to-face meetings with suspects. They hoped that these meetings would yield evidence of the crime.

In four of the cases no additional evidence gathering steps were used by the police. Existing messages became the language evidence in chapter 11 (David Dawson) and existing recorded language was the undercover evidence described in a prostitution sting involving a famous athlete, described in chapter 13. Existing written language in Senator Packwood's diaries also framed the evidence described in chapter 6 and in the written statement in chapter 10 (Jim Keckoff).

Even though the alleged victims did the talking, the confrontation calls and meetings were carefully orchestrated and monitored by the police, so any potential or actual flaws in the evidence are the ultimate responsibility of the monitoring intelligence gatherers, while the intelligence analysis of these calls and meetings is the responsibility of the prosecutors. Since no additional evidence was gathered by the police in these cases, the responsibility for making an indictment fell on the shoulders of the prosecutor alone.

Following Godfrey and Harris (1971), the two crucial steps in such cases are called intelligence gathering and intelligence analysis (Shuy 1990, 125–126, 2011). Normally the intelligence is gathered by law enforcement officers, whose job it is to discover facts that provide information for a prosecutor's eventual intelligence analysis to determine whether a person is either guilty or innocent. Commonly one of the first places the defense can focus its energy is on the nature and quality of the evidence collected by these law enforcement officers, whether taped meetings, phone calls, or written material.

It is the proper role of the intelligence gatherer to collect evidence that will provide true and conclusive proof. Deciding whether or not it does this is the job of the prosecutor—the intelligence analyst—who must carefully review and evaluate the intelligence gathered by law enforcement and then conclude whether or not to go forward with an indictment. Sometimes, unfortunately, intelligence gatherers confuse their proper fact-finding role with that of the prosecutor's proper role of determining its legal value. The resulting problem is that the intelligence gatherers can contaminate the very evidence they are gathering. This problem is found not only in electronically recorded efforts to capture guilt in police interviews, but also in the subsequent written police reports. Interviewers can be so intent on eliciting guilt that their fact-finding efforts are accompanied by repeated accusations, harassment, and other verbal behaviors similar to those sometimes found in courtroom cross-examinations. Police reports can fall into the same trap, reporting or creating statements that the police may have thought they heard. When this happens, they too can be vigorously disputed by alert attorneys.

Because sexual misconduct usually cannot be caught as it is happening, the prosecution relies heavily on after-the-fact accusations of victims and on the testimony of witnesses. In order to support this intelligence, sometimes the police also ask the complainant to engage in confrontation calls or meetings with suspects in order to try to get them to admit their crimes and confess or apologize. The cases described here evidenced several important problems: inadequate electronic recordings, inadequate transcriptions of recordings, inadequate police interviewing, inadequate management of recorded confrontation calls and meetings, inadequate use of one-way communication evidence, and misinterpreting the actions and intentions of both the complainants and suspects. All of these point directly to inadequate intelligence gathering and inadequate intelligence analysis.

PROBLEMS WITH INADEQUATE ELECTRONIC RECORDING OF EVIDENCE

Perhaps the most egregious example of inadequate intelligence gathering is illustrated in the case of the famous athlete (chapter 13), where the police recording was so technically flawed that the transcribers had to resort to guessing badly at the actual words on the taped transmission. Nor were the accompanying police reports very helpful to the prosecution, for their imprecision about distances between the athlete and the undercover policewoman led to questions of whether she could actually have heard what was allegedly said to her. Further factual disputes arose about where and when the athlete's car stopped, and about how the athlete could have waved at the woman with his left hand (she was standing on the curb to his right) through a halfway rolled down car window on the passenger side, and how she could verify that he waved to her "in a beckoning manner." All of this opened to door to criticism, if not impeachment of the report.

The failure of electronic equipment also made the prosecutor's case against Sheriff Preston (chapter 5) much more difficult than it might have been had the audio track been clearer. All the police had to go on was the voice-activated audio recording, which cut in and out throughout the conversation and failed to be improved even by professional enhancement techniques.

PROBLEMS WITH INADEQUATE TRANSCRIPTIONS OF THE LANGUAGE EVIDENCE

The transcriber's failure to note Sam Graybo's (chapter 7) long sigh accompanying his eventual "yes" admission of guilt was a serious transcription omission. This sigh indicated that he was so frustrated by repeatedly denying his accuser's repeated accusations that he finally just gave up in an effort to end his torment. The prosecutor's transcriber also added the word "in" when no such word was audible in the words of Sheriff Williams's accuser (chapter 5) when she told him on tape, "you went down *in* my pants."

And, of course, the creative but faulty transcription of the audiotape of the famous athlete (chapter 13) was the most egregious of all, as it converted his audible "wanna dance for an hour" to "how much for an hour" and his "have a little fun for about an hour" to "some head and a little fuckie for one hundred dollars." One would like to believe that government-sponsored and prepared transcripts of such conversations would be done accurately, objectively, and without bias.

Not all transcriptions of language can be attributed to law enforcement. Senator Packwood's secretary (chapter 6) also made multiple transcription errors as she tried to commit the senator's daily tape-recorded diary to paper. She quite naturally had considerable problems with determining whether the senator's quoted or reconstructed diary actually represented what people said on any given day. This only compounded the problems for any later analysis, since the senator may have only imagined these passages or constructed them to suit his own position on various topics. In other words, transcript accuracy was doubtful in two ways: whether the senator recalled the passage with any degree of accuracy and whether his secretary transcribed it accurately. Such doubts made using his diary entries dicey for both the investigating Senate Ethics Committee and for the Department of Justice, who may have had their own schemas for interpreting them. One source of doubt comes from the fact that secretaries are used to taking drafts written by supervisors and trying to make sense of them. Their own schemas are at work in this, often based on their own perceptions of not only what the tape said, but also on their perceived need to correct small (or even large) errors, including the tenses of verbs and the use of modals. Senator Packwood's secretary also tended to err in leaving out some of what she heard and adding things she didn't hear, possibly as a way of trying to be helpful to her boss.

Even transcripts constructed by the prosecution and defense in criminal cases where oral language must be presented to juries can suffer from the same problems. I have found that government-produced transcripts in many criminal trials tend to have errors that favor the prosecution and transcripts produced by the defense often contain errors that favor the defendant. Small things can be added, omitted, or changed, making all the difference. The need for a well-trained linguist to produce or correct transcripts is obvious for both sides of a case (Shuy 1993, 37–38, 1998, 126, 2005, 46–48, 126–127). Nor are nonprofessional transcribers the only source of such errors. Walker (1990, 203–244), herself a former court reporter who later became a linguist, describes the shocking failures of certified court reporters as they try to transcribe court events accurately, along with the effects of these transcription errors on the actual legal events.

PROBLEMS WITH INADEQUATE INTERVIEWING OF SUSPECTS AND WITNESSES

The police interviews of the complainant and the corroborating witness in Ken Martin's case (chapter 9) were faulty in many ways. From the very beginning, rather than being an objective fact-finding event, the interview of the complainant revealed many of the characteristics of a therapy session, assuring the alleged victim that Ken "wouldn't get away with it," telling the alleged victim "you were brainwashed" and "he manipulated you," all at the very start of the interview, but also similarly interspersed throughout it. There was no skeptical neutrality, minimum of interpretation, or apparent concern about possible interviewer interference in collecting factual and accurate intelligence to be used later by the intelligence analyst. The alleged fact finder was clearly on the complainant's side from the start and accepted her account as totally true, and even though the statements she heard were sometimes contradictory, these contradictions went unchallenged. When the corroborating witness faltered for words, the interviewer spoon fed them to her, especially when the suggested words pointed to Martin's guilt. In addition, the interviewer made no effort to clarify the contradictory statements made by both the complainant and the witness, apparently assuming that the most accusatory statements trumped the most benign ones.

In the police interview of Raul Sanchez (chapter 8) the investigator accused the suspect more than twenty times, but Sanchez still insisted on his innocence, and even cooperatively volunteered information that was not asked of him (e.g., that he was an illegal alien). He volunteered to be medically examined and even suggested witnesses at the party that the police had not (and did not) interview. Despite this, the intelligence analyst still considered this Sanchez's admission and confession. During the police interview of Lena's mother, the police threatened her that if she did not admit that her ex-husband had molested Lena, Child Protection Services would take her younger children away from her. This was not a pretty picture.

PROBLEMS WITH INADEQUATE CONFRONTATION CALL EVIDENCE

Realizing that their interviews with witnesses required further substantiation, in five of the cases described here the police intelligence gatherers also made use of the intelligence gathering strategy of the confrontation call, in which victims make phone calls to the suspects, trying to get them to acknowledge, admit, and confess their offenses. When the complainants couldn't elicit an admission, they tried for an apology, which, if given, might nail down a conviction. Most complainants in such cases are not skilled at eliciting confessions, even though the police coach them before the calls are made and sit beside them while they are talking, making suggestions as the calls progress.

This confrontation call and confrontation meeting strategy is very similar to the four-step approach advocated for use by law enforcement officers as they interrogate suspects, in which interviewers are encouraged to follow this pattern:

1. Let the suspect bring up whatever topics he or she wants, in the hope that as the suspect will talk freely and self-generate guilt. If the suspect doesn't say anything inculpatory, move to step 2.
2. Vaguely mention the offense, without saying anything specific. Drop hints and use vague references such as "it happened" or "why did you do it?" If the suspect interprets these vague references as relating to his or her offense, the suspect might bite. If not, move to step three.
3. Retell part of the event in question, still being as vague as possible, hoping the suspect will expand on his or her alleged role in the event. If the suspect still doesn't implicate him- or herself, the stronger measures of step 4 are needed.
4. Be explicit and specific. Now the earlier vagueness, general referencing, hints, and retellings come together in a more specific accusation that the suspect can either agree with or deny.

It is rare, however, that the complainants in the confrontation calls and meetings have enough patience or skill to use step 1. Instead, they tend to begin with step 2, vagueness while dropping hints, and step 3, the partial retelling strategy. The cases of Dr. Desai (chapter 4), Sam Graybo (chapter 7), Raul Sanchez (chapter 8), and especially Ken Martin (chapter 9) illustrate how the confrontation callers did this.

The difficulty of succeeding in the effort to elicit guilt during confrontation calls is illustrated by the fact that it took six such calls to satisfy the prosecutor that he had enough to indict Dr. Desai (chapter 4), four such calls to indict Ken Martin (chapter 9), two such calls to indict Sam Graybo (chapter 7), and two such calls to indict Raul Sanchez (chapter 8). As noted earlier, the fact that follow-up calls had to be made gives evidence that the calls preceding the final one did not satisfy the prosecutor's need for an indictment.

Those callers who finally managed to make their accusations somewhat clear and specific (step 4) met with strong denials, with the exception of Dr. Desai (chapter 4) and Sam Graybo (chapter 7), both of whom were so worn down by the caller's repeated accusations that they were willing to agree to virtually anything in order to bring the conversations to an end.

Although the cases of Dr. Berger (chapter 3), Sheriff Williams (chapter 5), Stephen Ray (chapter 12), and the famous athlete (chapter 13) involved tape-recorded meetings rather than confrontation calls, they produced problems for the prosecution that were similar to those of the confrontation calls.

PROBLEMS WITH ONE-WAY COMMUNICATIONS AS EVIDENCE

The case of David Dawson (chapter 11) is somewhat unique because the evidence used against him was what can be called one-way communication. I have worked on cases in the past in which only one of the two speakers' voices could be heard. This happens with telephone calls, for example, when only one of the voices is capable of being transcribed. This poses a serious problem for both the prosecution and the defense, for both sides have to infer or guess what the unheard party said. Inferences and guesswork are far cries from good evidence. It is dangerous to conclude "he must have said X," for doing so lays wide open the opportunity to challenge and cross-examine. Such inferences, of course, are also highly subject to the later listener's or later reader's schema about the entire event.

The recorded evidence used against David Dawson was a one-way series of phone messages and emails that went unanswered by his accuser. Therefore we are left with only half of a conversation, much like the unrecorded half of telephone conversations noted earlier. To the several times that David wrote or said "I'm sorry," later listeners had to guess what he was actually sorry about. They also had to guess what David meant when he said "what happened was my fault." The police, guessing what he referred to, reasoned that David was sorry for using force. Based only on what David said, this reasoning had no merit. It was an inference, and inferences seldom go unchallenged in the courtroom. If Ginny had answered David's phone calls and emails, the police might have learned much more than they got from this one-way communication.

PROBLEMS WITH ASSESSING INTENTIONS AND MOTIVES OF COMPLAINANTS

It is not the linguist's task to identify the intentions underlying the accusations made in law cases, and I certainly make no claim to establish intentions here, but the participants' schemas revealed by the language they use certainly suggest clues to their intentions, whether the intelligence gatherers and analysts thought so or not. It would not be too difficult to hypothesize the possible intentions of the complainants in nine of these eleven cases. The intentions of the complainants are not apparent in the cases of Dr. Berger (chapter 3) and Sam Graybo (chapter 7), but in the following cases the police did not explore the following possible intentions:

Chapter 4, Dr. Desai: The complainant intended to put the blame on the doctor so that she could make peace with her husband about having an abortion without telling him. Additionally, the complainant wanted the doctor to marry her after her husband divorced her.

Chapter 5, Sheriff Williams: The complainant intended to pin a crime on the sheriff so that her friend, the assistant sheriff, could replace him.

Chapter 6, Senator Packwood: If the government could convict him of a felony crime of improper dealings with lobbyists, this would support the charges of sexual misconduct. Convicting a political celebrity would bring credit to the Department of Justice.

Chapter 8, Raul Sanchez: The complainant intended to get even with her stepfather for not permitting her to date an older man.

Chapter 9, Ken Martin: The charges were motivated by his angry ex-wife, who knew that her daughter was angry with her stepfather about other matters and encouraged her to charge him with sexual misconduct as a way of getting even with him.

Chapter 10, Jim Keckoff: The motives of his stepdaughter, who lived with him in the same house, were unclear, but her intention could have been that since they were far from friendly, she was trying to get him out of her life and home.

Chapter 11, David Swanson: The complainant had second thoughts about how far she let him go on their date and suddenly became embarrassed and remorseful after her roommate came in and saw them in bed together. Her intention was to excuse her embarrassment by shifting blame onto him.

In the case of the famous athlete (chapter 13), the intentions of the police are at least suspicious. Believing they had caught a celebrity in the prostitution sting, the police intended to create facts to gain notoriety for their case and credit for the department.

My point here is not that linguists could prove these intentions, or that they should even try. But intentions are closely related to the schemas of the complainants and should be carefully considered by intelligence analysts. The possible intentions of participants provide part of the overall context in which such cases are brought and tried.

Solan (2009, 517–535) argues, convincingly I believe, that humans are more likely to attribute intent to those whose actions lead to bad results than to those whose actions lead to good results. He argues that we are somehow designed to lash out at wrongdoers out of a strong sense of morality and that such intent is built into our thinking without out even recognizing it. The reason for this is that our bias toward blame results from our tendency to expect good. When a bad event is reported, it is only natural for us to believe that the reported act is not only true, but is also intentional.

It may be easier to understand the intentions of the complainants in these cases, however, than the intentions of the police intelligence gatherers and the prosecution intelligence analysts. When the police hold a schema that a suspect has committed a wrongful act, as most of these did, it is only natural for the police also to believe that the intentions of the suspect are equally bad, and conversely, it is difficult for the police to believe that the suspect could possibly have had innocent intentions. Police, on the other hand, have a moral and practical duty, as law officers investigating a potential crime, to take a neutral stance as they gather and analyze the facts in an investigation, including the possible intentions of the participants. A bad act may have been reported, but the alleged bad actor's intentions cannot be dismissed merely because a bad act occurred.

Solan (2009) goes on to point out that in ordinary speech it would be odd for speakers to attribute good intentions to every act they report, such as "I intentionally went to the store today." We don't say things like that because, following Grice's cooperative principle (1975, 45), we assume that good and normal things are done intentionally and with a purpose, without having to mark it as such, and then we evaluate what is said against this underlying assumption. When we do mark an everyday event like this explicitly, we are highlighting our intention as different from this natural assumption.

Since our legal system is likely to expect good actions and disapprove of bad ones, the police and prosecution can be easily blinded to the possibility that the suspects involved in bad acts actually had good intentions. Such expectations helped prevent the law officers from seeing the possibility that Sam Graybo (chapter 7), Raul Sanchez (chapter 8), Ken Martin (chapter 9), Jim Keckoff (chapter 10), and David Dawson (chapter 11) could possibly have had good intentions in their own self-reported accounts of their bad acts. Perhaps the most egregious assumption of bad acts was in the case of the famous athlete (chapter 13), where the very context of a prostitution sting operation blinded the police so much that they mistranscribed what was actually said in the recorded exchange with the police decoy.

SUMMING UP

I am happy to say that not all law enforcement is as lax in the use of law enforcement tools and techniques as the cases in this book illustrate. No doubt there are many examples of proper intelligence gathering carried out by law enforcement officers. However, forensic linguists seldom get the opportunity to witness proper police procedures in action. We are not called upon for help unless the retaining attorneys have reason to believe that procedures were inadequately carried out. Most often it is the linguist's task to analyze the language that is used in questionable cases like these. It is my hope that law enforcement will be motivated to avoid the problems discussed and illustrated in this book. At the same time, I hope that other linguists and students of linguistics will be heartened and perhaps even instructed by the use of the linguistic analytical procedures used in these eleven cases. Although this book represents a range of sexual misconduct cases, by no means does it represent them all. As in all forensic linguistic work, we analyze the language evidence we are given; nothing more, nothing less.

[15]

USING LINGUISTIC TOOLS IN SEXUAL MISCONDUCT CASES

While the forensic sciences seem to be focusing on smaller and smaller evidence units to solve crimes, such a DNA and fingerprints, I argue that legal evidence involving language should be moving in exactly the opposite direction, starting the analysis with the larger language units before even trying to deal with the smaller ones. In *The Language of Perjury Cases* (2011) I suggested this very approach, observing that larger language units provide the necessary context for examining smaller language units. This is somewhat parallel to a physician making a holistic medical examination of a patient before making a particularistic analysis of an isolated part of a patient's malfunctioning body or mind. The pattern for analysis that I presented in that book is that of an inverted triangle, beginning with large language units at the top and proceeding down the inverted triangle to the smaller ones, as follows:

1. Identify the *speech event* represented by the language evidence by asking "what is the event in which this language occurs?"
2. Identify the *schemas* of the participants as revealed by the language they use.

3. Identify the participants' conversational agendas as these are revealed by the *topics* they introduce and recycle.
4. Identify the participants' agendas as revealed by their *responses* to the topics brought up by others.
5. Identify the *speech acts* used by the participants in order to determine whether or not they are felicitous.
6. Identify the participants' use or nonuse of the *cooperative principle* in order to determine the strength and validity of their contributions.
7. Identify the *conversational strategies* used by the participants in order to determine their potential effect on the responses of others.
8. Identify uses of the *recency principle* used by the participants in order to determine whether or not they are actually replying to the points made by the other speaker.
9. Identify the *grammatical and phonological ambiguity* and significance in the language of the participants in order to determine whether context can resolve the ambiguity.
10. Identify the *semantic ambiguity* and significance of words and phrases used by the participants in order to determine how and if such ambiguity was or could be resolved.

One of the temptations of both the prosecution and defense lawyers is to be unduly enamored of the smaller language units, such as words and phrases that are near the bottom of the list, possibly because these most easily and quickly capture their attention and are more discrete, much like smoking guns.

Sometimes these smaller language features are significant, and indeed may even turn out to be smoking guns, but more often than not they need to be viewed in the larger communicative context, not just in the parts of isolated sentences where they occur. That is precisely why I have suggested that prosecutors, defense lawyers, and linguists begin their analyses at the top of the list, beginning with a clear understanding of the large language units, such as the speech event, the schemas of the participants, and their agendas as revealed by their topics and responses, as well as with the speech acts and language strategies the participants introduce and use. Smaller language units, such as words, phrases, and sentences can be significant, of course, but they should be analyzed according to how they are nested into the overall context and how they relate to the larger language units. For example, when a suspect says "I'm sorry," the expression is meaningless without knowing what the suspect is sorry about. This often can be discerned from their contextualized schemas, conversational agendas, and speech acts. Yet, "I'm sorry," which many of the suspects said in the cases described in this book, looks like a smoking gun to prosecutors who fail to dig deeper into the total context of the conversations.

I should also make it clear that the language evidence in individual law cases does not always call for detailed analysis of all ten of the language units mentioned earlier. This list is more a reminder about the general direction to take than it is a firm step-by-step process that will fit all data. Each case offers its own evidence, and it is up to the analyst, whether lawyer or linguist, to make use of only the most appropriate and productive tools. The eleven cases described here are no exception. In fact, some of these language units turned out to be less salient in a few of these cases, but in most of the cases it would have benefited both the prosecution and defense to begin their analyses with the larger units of the speech event, schema, and speech acts.

Although the language unit comprised of conversational strategies, which played an important role in the cases I described in *Creating Language Crimes* (2005) also can be useful in sexual misconduct cases, this language unit played only a minimal role in the language evidence discussed here. The reason may be due the fact that the language evidence in most of these cases is more restricted to the form of questions and answers. This is characteristic of police interviews and electronically recorded verbal duels by participants about whether or not the accusations they made were valid. Perhaps for the same reasons, use of the recency principle, a language unit that has seemed to be so valuable in many other criminal and civil lawsuits, was not as evident in the cases described in this book. On the whole, however, I have reason to believe that this sequential top-down analysis of the ten language units is an effective way for both attorneys and linguists to proceed as they deal with their case evidence. The following sections reprise how this approach worked in these eleven cases.

SPEECH EVENT ANALYSIS

The first thing for prudent prosecutors and defense attorneys to do when they review the language evidence in any case, including sexual misconduct cases, is to be aware of and understand what the particular speech event is. As Gumperz (1990, 9) points out, speech events are recurring occasions that have "tacitly understood rules of preference, unspoken conventions as to what counts as valid and what information may or may not be introduced." The speech event therefore predicts the parameters of what participants can be expected to say. For example, the way the participants talk during such events reflects the power asymmetry that lurks beneath the surface under the appearance of equality. The nature of the speech event tends to dictate how the participants are allowed to talk with each other.

Four different speech events are identified in these eleven cases: the confrontation event, the police interview event, the diary event, and the one-way communication event (which obviously included no response at all from one of the communicators).

The confrontation speech event

The speech event of the confrontation calls in chapters 4, 7, 8, 9, and 12 and the confrontation meetings in chapters 3 and 5 were tape-recorded oral confrontations. These confrontations differed from many confrontation speech events, however, because as these confrontations began, only one of the two participants in each of them was initially aware that these conversations were actually going to be confrontations. In most cases, as they became aware of the nature of the conversations, the communication turned into arguments, disputes, or disagreements. The exception to this was the confrontation meeting of Sheriff Preston (chapter 5), who, as both the complainant and supervising policeman laughingly noted at the end of the recording, never figured out what the discussion was all about and therefore never understood the purpose and nature of the confrontation. In the confrontation calls in the cases of Dr. Desai (chapter 4) and Sam Graybo (chapter 7), the calls ended with their apparent frustrated and begrudging agreement with the callers' accusations, because they simply gave up trying to convince the callers that they actually were denying the multiply repeated accusations. Their eventual agreements, as was pointed out in these chapters, could be understood as pseudo-agreements rather than evidence that they actually confessed to the accusations.

The police interview speech event

Police interviews can be characterized by their rigid question-and-answer format that is controlled by questioners, with few if any opportunities for responders to ask their own questions. Unlike normal conversations, there can be no mutual exchange of information. The police interview also reflects the experiences of courtroom witnesses, including expert witnesses, when they testify at depositions and in trials. It is as unusual for suspects to volunteer information in police interviews as it is for witnesses to volunteer information in depositions. In fact, witnesses are urged not to do so by their retaining attorneys.

As noted throughout this book, police interviews are, by definition, fact-finding events with suspects or witnesses in which the interviewer is supposed to be objective and neutral until such time as it is clear that the interviewee has revealed strong and clear indications of guilt. At that point the interview turns into an interrogation, a more outwardly hostile questioning period in which harsh questioning takes place.

Authorities on police interrogations are in general agreement about how to define the interview and the interrogation. Yeschke (1987, 25) describes interviewing as "a dynamic human interaction having the purpose of collecting truthful data to be used for mature decision-making and just action-taking." He contrasts the interview with the interrogation, defining the latter as "a face-to-face meeting with the distinct task of gaining an admission of confession in a real or apparent violation of law, policy, regulation or other restriction."

O'Hara and O'Hara (1988, 94) do not make confession the distinguishing characteristic of police interviews, saying, "interviews are conducted with persons believed to possess knowledge that is of official interest to the investigator" whereas interrogations are given to persons "suspected of having committed an offense." Aubry and Caputo (1980, 94) agree with Yeschke (1987) that the purpose of an interrogation is to obtain "an admission of guilt from an individual who has committed a crime," although they also point out that the interview and interrogation are both "techniques for securing information." Royal and Schutt (1976, 116) say that obtaining a confession is the goal of the interrogation rather than the interview.

Gudjonsson (1993, 8) describes the four standard phases of police interviews:

1. Phase 1, orientation
   a. purpose of the interview stated
   b. introducing participants
   c. legal requirements fulfilled
2. Phase 2, listening
   a. subject gives free recall account
3. Phase 3, questions and answers
   a. subject asked specific questions
4. Phase 4, advice
   a. reading through statement
   b. signing statement
   c. subject informed of further actions
   d. interview session terminated

Phases 1 and 4 are standard boilerplate. During phase 2 the interviewer mainly listens while the subject tells what happened. The police then use this information to formulate their questions in phase 3.

The phase 3 questions are to discover and resolve ambiguities and uncertainties mentioned during phase 2, to get the subject to expand with details, to fill in gaps missed or overlooked by the subjects in phase 2, and to obtain specific information, some of which might be incriminating or exculpatory. Note that there is a definite shift in participant power from phase 2 to phase 3. In phase 2 the police listen while the subject is in control of what is said, whereas in phase 3 the control and power shifts to the interviewer, who asks the questions while the subject is expected to answer.

Based on what authorities say about the police interview, it is reasonable to expect the gathering of intelligence to begin with objective, fact-finding intentions. Only when it has become reasonably evident to the interviewer that the suspect may indeed be guilty or untruthful do the interviewers switch directions to the accusations and challenges that are characteristic of interrogations. Such evidence can come from the subject's self-contradictory testimony or from conflicts with previously known and established facts. The switch from interview to interrogation does not come, however, from the subjects' contradictory statements based on information given by complainants or other witnesses, for if this happens the questioner is likely to move out of the territory assigned to the intelligence gatherer and into the role assigned to the intelligence analyst, the prosecutor. In such cases, the police interviewers can be accused of trying to accomplish the entire legal process at one time. However, their job is only to obtain needed or missing information. In confession statements this includes exactly what the suspect is confessing to (Wrightsman and Kassin 1993, 6), for "it is far better to fulfill the role of one who is seeking the truth" (Inbau, Reid, and Buckley 1986, 36).

Thus the structure of the police interview speech event is of considerable interest to linguists because it often varies from having the form of an interview to being an interrogation. Linguistic analysis can point out how and when it shifts structurally.

There were likely police interviews in the other cases described in this book, but in only two of the cases did the attorneys provide me with the police interviews of suspects and witnesses for analysis—the cases of Raul Sanchez (chapter 8) and Ken Martin (chapter 9). I can suppose that there were interviews in other cases, but if so, they were not given to me to analyze.

The identification of schemas (see below) plays an important role in the questioning of victims, suspects, and witnesses. The schemas of the police who questioned Raul Sanchez (chapter 8) and Ken Martin (chapter 9) gave clear language evidence that they had abandoned any interest in objective fact-finding from the very start, believing the complainants' accusations to be true without checking them out. There was nothing in any of the interviews conducted by the police in these cases that remotely resembled the phase 2 listening part of the interview outlined by Gudjonsson (1993). Even worse, the interviewer-turned-interrogators' written reports did not always accurately represent what was said in their electronically recorded oral interviews. The highly conflicting reports of the witnesses to the alleged crime were so inconsistent and contradictory that they were not useful to the police. The police had only the accusations to go on until they got the complainants to make confrontation calls to or have confrontation meetings with the suspects in order to provide evidence to support their complaints.

The diary as a speech event

The major evidence in the case of Senator Packwood (chapter 6) consisted of the 3,200 pages of daily entries in his diary. Diaries are normally written for the future reference of the writer alone. They are private, usually informal records for diarists to refer to later if they wish. At the same time, they are reflections of what the writer was thinking about, hoping for, and feeling at a specific time. There is no particular need for diaries to be precise or even accurate, for in this regard they are unlike history, biography, or academic articles. Diaries are unplanned and assume contextual information that later outside readers might not know. As evidence in a law case, diaries have characteristics that may be helpful, including the discoverable schemas of the writer, but they can have questionable usefulness as evidence of wrong doing.

The one-way communication speech event

There are many types of oral one-way communication speech events, including classroom lectures, sermons, and political speeches. By "one-way" I mean that the major, if not the entire flow of oral communication goes from one person to others with no institutionalized feedback provided. Listeners, of course, may shout out their objection or approval, say "amen," and hiss, cheer, or otherwise react, but these are not substantive or discussable verbal responses to what was said by the speaker. More than anything, there is none of the specific statement–response dyadic exchange that characterizes two-way communication. The one-way phone and email communications of David Dawson (chapter 11) illustrate this because they provided the police with their most crucial evidence against him.

Written language is normally a one-way communication, with writers isolated in time and space from any immediate responses about what they write. One can write a letter back to someone who has first written you, but the resulting communication is not the immediate point-by-point, question-and-answer, same-time, same-place type of dyadic communication that characterizes oral dialogue. There are channels in which two-way written communication comes close to oral two-way communication, such as texting and dialogue journal writing (Staton et al. 1988), but even these are not immediate in time and space.

The one-way written statement made by Jim Keckoff (chapter 10) was a statement the police asked him to write about the night of the event when he was arrested. Even though he described the crucial event of feeling his stepdaughter's breast as a hypothesis for accidentally touching her, the police considered it an admission of his intention to do so. One can only wonder what might have happened if Keckoff had been asked about this in an interview, where he could have explained his hypothesis further. The one-way written communication offered no such opportunity. The one-way communication found in Senator Packwood's diary (chapter 6) contains the same lack of response information, among the other problems noted in that chapter.

One may wonder why the law treats written evidence as more final and conclusive than the spoken word. One answer is in Tiersma's book, *Parchment Paper Pixels* (2010), where he describes the gradual changes in law from its oral beginnings to its current, almost total reliance on written language to represent the facts of a law case. Once something is committed to writing, any earlier oral versions become virtually irrelevant and forgotten. In Keckoff's case what he wrote, despite being a mere hypothesis, was taken as his written confession.

The one-way communication speech event has its own advantages, one of which is that senders can maintain the floor and can organize their presentations in any way they wish, with no interruptions. Their greatest disadvantage is the possibility of their being vague and unclear, leading to interpretations that were not intended by the writer. Still, they provide evidence of only one side of the information needed by intelligence analysts.

SCHEMA ANALYSIS

After recognizing the importance of the speech event, the next large language unit to consider is schema analysis. Schemas are the expectations people have about what is said, based on what they already know and understand about their world. Schemas are something like prerecorded scripts that people have in their heads that they then call upon as they interpret and try to understand new information that comes to them. Somewhat like triggers, they facilitate communication, but in other ways they can also distort what is heard and lead to erroneous inferences and understandings.

It is perhaps understandable for law enforcement officers to begin with a schema of the alleged offender's guilt. The alleged victim has told them this and often the police have no particular reason to doubt the veracity of the complaint. As with all schema, however, it is necessary for intelligence gatherers to try to hold their schemas of guilt in check until they can either verify or challenge what was told to them. Unchecked schemas can blind police, prosecutors, and defense attorneys, causing them to overlook evidence that may prove to be contradictory. Schemas of the participants in conversations can also blind them to what the other speaker means.

The case of the famous athlete (chapter 13) is a good example of problems growing from the law enforcement officers' schema of guilt. The police were so convinced that the athlete was soliciting a prostitute that their schema seriously influenced their ability to hear what was actually said on the tape recording of his conversation on the street corner. Likewise, the prosecutor's schema in his interview of Jim Keckoff (chapter 10) led him to interpret the suspect's hypothetical explanation about how he ended up in bed with his stepdaughter as an admission that he did so intentionally.

Victims and suspects can fall into the same trap. In the cases of Sheriff Preston (chapter 5) and Stephen Ray (chapter 12), the suspects and the accusers held very different schemas about what their alleged offenses were. During the confrontation efforts of their complainants, Dr. Berger (chapter 3), Sam Graybo (chapter 7), Raul Sanchez (chapter 8), Ken Martin (chapter 9), and David Dawson (chapter 11) also had very different schemas about what their accusers were talking about. When intelligence analysts fail to figure out that the parties are on very different schema wavelengths, a correct understanding of the taped conversations can go very wrong.

The prosecutor's schema about Dr. Desai (chapter 4) was fueled not only by the accusation, but also by extracontextual factors that arose out of the doctor's past legal charges that he had burned the fetuses resulting from abortions he had performed several years earlier. And it is not irrelevant that in his conservative community, any physician who performs abortions begins with an unfavorable schema of the public as well as of the police. This schema may have helped blind the prosecutor to the fact that in the confrontation tape conversations of the doctor with his accuser, they were talking about very different things. The prosecutor in Dr. Berger's case (chapter 3) also apparently overlooked the fact that the schema of the doctor was actually to try to get his patient to have sex with him willingly, not as a quid pro quo in exchange for writing a letter for her.

Whether the differing schemas were those of the victims or those of the police intelligence gatherer and intelligence analyst seemed to make little difference in the decision to prosecute. The intelligence analysts' responsibility should have been to recognize and account for these schemas as they decide whether or not to prosecute.

AGENDA ANALYSIS AS REVEALED BY TOPICS AND RESPONSES

One of the language units that appeared somewhat less frequently in these eleven cases is identification of the participants' agendas as revealed by the topics they introduce and by their responses to the topics of others. The participants' agendas are usually more useful in cases where large amounts of continuous speech are the evidence, such as the language used in bribery, money laundering, or narcotics transactions while the speakers talk with each other.

Typically topic analysis charts contain all of the individually introduced and recycled topics in a given text as a way of visually illustrating the clues about what was on the speaker's mind. Response analysis isolates the most critical passages and places them side by side with the statements of the other speaker. This approach is particularly helpful to juries who might otherwise lose sight of the context of who says what to whom. Together, the topics and responses focus on the clues to the conversational agendas of the speakers. Such charts are often too long to be included in chapters of books, but they can be very useful for lawyers or for expert witness testimony at trial.

In the case of Dr. Berger (chapter 3) I modified this approach somewhat, lumping together all of the individually introduced topics into three thematic segments of the conversation. Since his patient recycled her quid pro quo topic many times during this meeting, there can be little doubt about what her agenda was.

When I analyzed Dr. Desai's case, I actually did a complete topic analysis for trial testimony purposes, but in chapter 4 I made only references to it, noting, for example, that the patient had introduced twice as many topics as the doctor, a sign of her conversational control. In the same way, in my discussion of Sam Graybo's case (chapter 7) I referred to my preceding analysis of the topics introduced by the participants along with Graybo's side-by-side responses to each topic, but I did not provide a chart of them all in this chapter. There is much that goes into a linguistic analysis that is not always practical to display in books such as this, and there is ample discussion of the procedure for carrying out topic–response analysis in my other publications. Other chapters, including the ones on Ken Martin (chapter 9) and David Dawson (chapter 11), also made use of topic analysis.

SPEECH ACT ANALYSIS

After the speech event and the schemas have been identified, the next large language unit to consider is the speech acts used by the participants. One primary definition of a speech act is that it is a locutionary act performed by a speaker who uses linguistic means with the intention of communicating a message to a listener. One simple and useful definition is that a speech act is a way of getting things done with language. Most people who are not versed in the notion of speech acts may suppose that the only units of communication are language sounds, words, and sentences. In truth, however, these smaller language units are inevitably put together to form larger speech act units. Since Searle (1969), linguists, including forensic linguists, have been using the linguistic unit of speech acts (Shuy 1993, 2008, 2010, 2011) and often find speech act analysis more helpful in determining possible clues to meanings than the smaller language units, especially when examining the language evidence in criminal law cases such as bribery, money laundering, defamation, and the sexual misconduct described in this book.

Language propositions have both a content (the body of the message) and an attitude (the orientation the speaker takes toward the speech act proposition). Propositional attitudes are identified with the speaker's various psychological states, including the following:

- The attitude that the belief represented in the proposition is true (speech acts of reporting, claiming, admitting, advising, warning).
- The attitude of desiring that the proposition be brought about (speech acts of requesting, ordering, pleading).
- The attitude of commitment to bring about the proposition (speech acts of promising, taking an oath, committing).
- The attitude of regret for bringing about the proposition (speech acts of regretting, apologizing, confessing).
- The attitude of intending to bring about the proposition (speech act of threatening).

Unless we understand the attitudinal orientation of a speech act, the words cannot always be properly understood by simple reference to only the words' literal meanings. Other matters, including the felicity of the expression and the context of the utterance also contribute to the intended meanings.

Even the Supreme Court of the United States recognized this in its 1973 opinion, *Bronston v. United States*, 409 U.S. 352, 353 (1973) (Solan and Tiersma 2005, 213). This dispute occurred when Bronston was asked at trial if he had bank accounts in Swiss banks. He answered, "No, sir." Then he was asked if he ever had an account there, to which he replied that his company had held an account there for about six months. Bronston's first answer was literally true, because although he once held a personal account in a Swiss bank, he did not hold one at the time he was asked. He was asked only if he held one, not if he had ever held one. The prosecutor then apparently tried to repair this and asked if Bronston had ever held one. To this, Bronston replied not with personal information, but rather about his company's past account in a Swiss bank. In short, Bronston did not provide any literally false information, but was convicted of perjury just the same. After the appellate court upheld his conviction, Bronston took it all the way to the U.S. Supreme Court, which then overturned his conviction, ruling that the perjury statute refers only to what the witness said, not to what he falsely implied, and that it was the prosecutor's responsibility to probe more deeply to resolve any possible ambiguity.

The meaning of an utterance is said to be literal if that utterance is composed only of the meanings of the words and phrases in accordance with syntactic conventions. The problem is that it is not always clear what the meanings of the words and phrases actually are. Words have a range of meanings and these meanings often depend on the context of the utterance. To this we need to add that the meanings of words and phrases also depend on the felicity conditions that regulate the acceptability of the speech acts in which they occur. For example, saying "I'm sorry" may look like a speech act of apologizing, but unless the utterance makes clear exactly what the speaker is sorry for,

"I'm sorry" simply fails as a true apology. We know the literal meaning of the words, "I'm" and "sorry," but their literal meanings do not constitute an apology without the further requirements and conditions required in the speech act of apologizing.

Six different speech acts played prominent roles in the analysis of the evidence in the cases described in this book: accusing, apologizing, admitting/confessing, denying, requesting directives, and conjecturing.

Accusing

Accusing falls into the larger speech act category of evaluatives, which includes many things, including regretting, praising, wishing, acknowledging, and complaining. Felicitous accusations that were made in the confrontation speech events described in this book would have the following characteristics:

1. The speaker has reason to believe that the listener played an active role in some action that the speaker disapproves of.
2. The speaker tells the listener that he, the listener, has played this active, offensive role.
3. The speaker specifically identifies what the offensive action was.
4. The listener is then given the opportunity to either agree with the speaker or disagree, offering his or her own counterarguments and defense.

As can be seen in the cases described in most of the chapters in this book, the accusations made by the complainants often failed to accomplish the requirements of a felicitous speech act of accusing, especially characteristic number 3, specifically identifying what the offensive action was. Accusing with only words such as "it" and "that" (as in chapters 5, 7, and 9, for example) leaves the door wide open for different understandings of the accusation.

Apologizing

As noted earlier, the "I'm sorry" responses of Dr. Desai (chapter 4), Sheriff Williams (chapter 5), David Dawson (chapter 11), and Stephen Ray (chapter 12) no doubt misled their prosecutors into believing that these suspects had actually apologized for their offensive acts. But even though each case had a different twist to the speaker's intentions, none of the men apologized for the act of which they had been accused. It behooves intelligence analysts to know the structure of a felicitous apology:

1. Mutual understanding and agreement about the act for which the apology is made.
2. Apologizer believes he is responsible for the offense.
3. The person apologized to is the person offended.
4. The offense is explicitly stated.
5. The apologizer promises not to commit the offense again.

As noted in the preceding chapters, the alleged apologies of these suspects missed the mark of being felicitous apologies in many ways, but especially in numbers 4 (identifying the offense), 2 (taking responsibility for it), and 1 (mutual understanding and agreement of the offense).

Admitting and confessing

The major purpose of the confrontation call is to elicit from the subject the speech acts of admitting and confessing the his or her guilt. I do not criticize this strategy, for it can be a very effective way to establish the guilt of a suspect. It may work very well in some sexual misconduct cases, but it cannot be considered a successful undercover strategy in the cases described in this book, largely because the intelligence gatherers and the intelligence analysts were either unable or unwilling to identify what the felicitous speech acts of admitting and confessing really were.

Admitting is an integral part of the speech act of asserting or affirming a proposition. The felicity conditions of admitting are

- The admitter has reasons for the truth of the proposition.
- It is obvious to both the admitter and listener that the listener knows what the admitter specifically is admitting.
- The proposition represents an actual state of affairs.

Representations of this speech act required special analysis in the cases of Dr. Desai (chapter 4) and Sam Graybo (chapter 7). After denying the accusations numerous times, both of these suspects finally uttered a mild and reluctant "yes" to their confrontation callers' accusations. Their answers apparently looked like admissions to the prosecutors, who took these admissions as confessions of guilt and subsequently pursued the cases at trial. The problem was, however, that a felicitous admission requires more than the propositional content.

As noted earlier, admitting also has to satisfy the requirements of the admitter's propositional attitude—the attitude that the propositional content is true, that the speaker desired that the content to be brought about, that the speaker intended to bring about that content, and that the speaker regretted bringing it about. There was nothing in the confrontation calls of Dr. Desai and Sam Graybo that could support these. Ignoring both the context of the calls and the failure of the men's statements to fulfill the requirements of the felicitous speech act of admitting, the prosecutors settled for the smoking gun of their final "yes" responses that were spoken in utter frustration by suspects who had vehemently denied their guilt throughout.

The speech acts of confessing and admitting are classic illustrations of the need for intelligence analysts to look first at the larger units of language before basing their cases on smaller units such as the allegedly smoking gun word represented by a subject's "yes" response. In the cases of Dr. Desai and Sam Graybo, the prosecution failed to address the speaker's propositional attitudes that were so essential to discovering the felicity of their speech acts.

Denying

Denying is a proposition with a negative assertion, fitting into the speech act category of assertives. The felicity conditions of a denial are

- the speaker has evidence (reasons, etc.) for the falsity of an assertion made by someone else,
- the speaker believes that the other person's assertion is not in the speaker's best interest,
- it is obvious to both the speaker and listener that the listener believes that his or her assertion is true,
- the speaker believes that the listener's assertion is false, and
- the speaker attempts to convince the listener that the listener's assertion is false.

The formal characteristics of the speech act of denying can be represented as strong, full, polite, and indirect. Examples include

Strong form	**Full form**	**Polite form**	**Indirect form**
You're a bald-face liar	I deny it	That's not true	(Person's name!)
You're dead wrong	I never did it	It's an error	That's silly

The strong form is vehement and is usually a threatening act because it addresses the accuser ("you") personally. The full form is less passionate but shifts the focus from the accuser to the person accused ("I"). The polite form shifts the topic from both the personal reference to the accuser ("you") and the accused ("I") to the accusation itself ("that" or "it"). The indirect form keeps the focus on the accusation, but treats it far less seriously. A common way to accomplish this is to say the accuser's name with an intonation contour beginning high, then dropping to low, indicating that the accusation is naive. Another way is to make light of the fact that an accusation was made in the first place ("that's silly"), indicating that the accusation does not even deserve comment.

Like other speech acts, denying has both a propositional content and a propositional attitude. The hearer must properly recognize the orientation that speakers hold when they deny something. Otherwise the denial can be greatly misunderstood. Participants in conversations usually understand the attitude of the responses to their accusations. In contrast, although later listeners, such as the police, lawyers, and juries, do not usually misinterpret the strong, full, and polite forms of denial, the indirect form can cause them some serious problems, as it did in the case of Raul Sanchez (chapter 8), when one of his many denials took the indirect form of saying the girl's name, "Lena," with the appropriate intonation contour of a high tone that drops to a low tone.

Then there is also the problem of how many times a person needs to deny the same accusation, which as far as I know has never been settled. Once they finally figured out what the caller was getting at, Sam Graybo (chapter 7) and Raul Sanchez (chapter 8) clearly denied their alleged offenses multiple times. On the other hand, Sheriff Preston (chapter 5), Ken Martin (chapter 9), Jim Keckoff (chapter 10), and David Dawson (chapter 11) never really had the chance to deny the accusations for various reasons, such as the interference caused by schema differences, the vague representations by their accusers, and, in Dawson's case, the one-way communication that left him without knowledge of what the accusation really was.

It is perhaps understandable that law enforcement officers and prosecutors have dealt with many suspects who falsely deny accusations of guilt. This generalization, however, cannot be an acceptable reason for them to discount the possibility that some defendants actually do tell the truth. For example, years ago, when I was conducting a workshop for federal drug enforcement officers, I pointed out that in undercover sting operations, when a suspect refuses an undercover officer's offer to buy or sell drugs, they just might possibly be innocent. At that point the hundred or so Drug Enforcement Agency (DEA) agents in the audience unanimously disagreed with me. They reasoned that if suspects are even present in a conversation about buying or selling illegal drugs, they are obviously guilty. This struck me as odd, because I had worked on cases in which an unsuspecting subject, suddenly accosted by an agent, was shocked by what the agent told him. There is certainly no infallible intuition about who will take the bait and who will not, but the agents' schema of guilt should not blind them to the possibility that there may be someone out there, despite the scenario constructed by law enforcement, who just might be there coincidentally.

More relevant to this book, the cases of Dr. Desai (chapter 4), Raul Sanchez (chapter 8), and Ken Martin (chapter 9) illustrate how the fallacy of the DEA agents' schema of guilt led prosecutors in these two cases to ignore protestations of innocence. Some of the police and prosecutors described here, like the DEA agents, could easily contaminate the intelligence gathering and analysis processes by assuming guilt despite the subject's clear use of the speech act of denying.

Requesting directives

Intelligence gatherers often employ the strategy of having the confrontation participant request a suspect give them directives (another speech act). I also do not criticize this law enforcement strategy because it sometimes elicits inculpatory responses by the suspect. On the other hand, sometimes it doesn't. The case of Dr. Desai (chapter 4) illustrates how the caller used this strategy. The problem with the evidence in this case was that the caller intermingled different requests for directives throughout, first asking the doctor to tell her what she should tell her husband regarding her previous abortion. Whether or not it was appropriate for a doctor to answer such questions (it's not illegal), he complied and made a suggestion about what she could tell him. In the caller's other request for a directive she asked the doctor for a directive to tell her that he is "ready" for her when she leaves her husband. To this request for a directive, he did not give an inculpatory response, replying instead, "Why should I be?" In the case of Raul Sanchez (chapter 8), his stepdaughter's requests for directives also yielded nothing useful for the prosecution. The complainant apparently was also well versed in how to use requests for directives in the case of Dr. Berger (chapter 3). After failing to get the doctor to agree to sexual favors in exchange for writing a support letter, she asked, "Where do we go from here?" and "Tell me what you'd be willing to do?" and other variants of this thirteen times in seven consecutive turns of talk. When she finally asked, "What do you want to do?" his answer is only an unconvincing "maybe."

Although requesting directives can be a useful strategy for confrontation callers to use, in these cases it clearly did not work the way the prosecution wanted it to.

Conjecturing

Conjecturing falls into the speech act categories of informatives and conclusives, the latter of which includes forecasts, predictions, and guesses. Conjecturing is much like the speech act of advising, in which the speaker presumes that the listener is unaware of the speaker's belief. But it differs from the speech act of claiming, in which the listener is aware of the speaker's belief but does not share it. In contrast, when speakers conjecture, they express belief in the possibility that something is the case. They guess, hypothesize, postulate, speculate, theorize, suggest, or suppose, often using modifiers such as "maybe," "possibly," "probably," or "perhaps." Conjecturing differs from other speech acts in which the speaker's assumptions are basically positive, using verbs like "assume," "believe," or "think."

The case of Jim Keckoff (chapter 10) best illustrates the use of the speech act of conjecturing when he said, "I *probably* rested my hand on Stacy's breast." He was offering a conjecture about what *may have* happened when he climbed into the wrong bed. It was not a confession statement, although the police incorrectly considered it one.

COOPERATIVE PRINCIPLE ANALYSIS

Whether or not one participant dominates and exhibits the most power in a conversation or interview, both speakers are expected to be cooperative, for otherwise there could be no meaningful conversation. The four maxims of conversational cooperation outlined by Grice (1975) are, in simplified terms,

- Be informative; say that which is required and no more than is required.
- Be relevant; don't wander off topic.
- Say what is true; be sincere.
- Be clear and orderly; avoid ambiguity and obscurity.

Even though this principle didn't play a large role in these eleven cases, it is a crucial language feature that speakers and listeners are often confused about. One example of violations of the cooperative principle is found in the police interviews of Raul Sanchez and the witnesses (chapter 8), when the interviewer frequently wandered off topic, said some unverifiable things, and was classically ambiguous and obscure.

One could also say that when the confronters kept on repeating their accusations over and over again, as in the cases of Dr. Desai (chapter 4) and Sam Graybo (chapter 7), they violated the maxim of informativeness by saying the same thing more than was cooperatively required. The very nature of confrontation calls and meetings could lead to the criticism of violating the maxim of being sincere, even though lack of sincerity may be the necessary hallmark of such procedures. Some of the accusers also violated the maxim of relevance by frequently wandering off topic, sometimes using a hit-and-run conversational strategy. Somehow, however, the suspects generally managed to keep their cool and struggled through these uncomfortable confrontations.

CONVERSATIONAL STRATEGIES ANALYSIS

Even though the language evidence in these cases did not provide many examples of the conscious or unconscious uses of the strategies of the participants, there were three that should be noted: the "don't accept denial" strategy, the "return to a safe haven" strategy, and the "hit-and-run" strategy.

The "don't accept denial" strategy

One conversational strategy found in the confrontation call and confrontation meeting is the refusal to accept multiple denials made by the defendants. The cases of Sam Graybo (chapter 7) and Raul Sanchez (chapter 8) illustrate how the callers used this strategy. I suspect that this strategy may have been borrowed from the handbooks on salesmanship: never accept a turndown from a customer and keep trying to sell the product no matter what happens.

The return to a safe haven strategy

In the case of Dr. Berger, his patient pursued two topics almost simultaneously throughout: her request for him to write a letter on her behalf and her attempts to get him to accept a quid pro quo by offering him sexual favors in exchange for his writing a supportive letter for her. When the doctor continuously stymied her quid pro quo, she used the "return to a safe haven" strategy three times, a common strategy in conversations. It works like this. When an effort to elicit agreement goes nowhere, the speaker retreats to the safe haven of a previous successful topic. This strategy was used by the confrontation caller in the case of Dr. Desai (chapter 4), when she regularly returned to the safe haven of her problem with her husband whenever the doctor rejected her requests for him to "be ready" for her.

The hit-and-run strategy

As noted in chapter 3, the confronter also used the "hit-and-run" strategy by first introducing an inculpatory topic to Dr. Berger, then abruptly changed the topic to a more benign one before the doctor could respond to her first topic. In other words, she hit and then quickly ran. He then responded to her second benign topic, at the same time also providing one of the few examples of the recency principle found in this book.

RECENCY PRINCIPLE ANALYSIS

The opportunity to analyze language for uses of the recency principle, which can be very helpful when analyzing continuous discourse in cases with large amounts of conversational evidence, is rather limited in cases where the type of language evidence is as specialized as it is in the cases described here. An example of the recency principle, used by Dr. Berger's patient (chapter 3), closely associates with the hit-and-run strategy, in that the doctor responded to the most recent statement of his patient, not to the first one that suggested his inculpation. In compound statements, people tend to reply to the most recent or last one in a series. Undercover agents in sting cases regularly use the recency principle (Shuy 2005).

ANALYSIS OF AMBIGUITY, SPECIFICITY, AND REFERENCING

As we consider the smaller units of language, such as grammar, words, and phrases, we are almost certain to see ambiguity play a role.

It is critical in any case involving spoken evidence, and often even in cases involving written evidence such as contract disputes and insurance policies (Shuy 2008). This happens especially when the participants have different schemas about the subjects they're discussing. Dr. Desai's language (chapter 4), for example, gave evidence that he thought his patient was referring to her efforts to hide her past abortion from her husband, while the patient actually was angling for the doctor to promise to get together with her romantically.

Similarly, when the complainant accosted Sheriff Preston (chapter 5), she introduced the issue by saying "we'd been carrying on and carrying on," which the sheriff apparently took to refer to what he considered to be the playful but improper touching and flirting that he willingly admitted. But her complaint to the police accused him of indecent exposure and assault and battery, something very different from his own perception of their past dalliance. Therefore, when he said "it will never happen again," the unspecified meaning of "it" in this sentence had very different meanings to the police. The tape-recoded conversation in evidence was replete with unspecified indexicals such as "this" and "that" and with unclear pronoun references such as "it," "she," and "her," none of which could be referentially identified in their talk. What the sheriff agreed to keep secret was their mutual fooling around, not the sexual misconduct claimed in his indictment. Grammatical and lexical referencing often goes hand in hand with schemas.

The different schemas of the participants also led to many ambiguities in the case of Sam Graybo (chapter 7). Graybo thought the girl's mother wanted him to assure her daughter that her nightmares in which Graybo performed sex acts on her were really only bad dreams and that she had no reason to be worried. The girl's mother encouraged and nurtured Graybo's schema throughout their two conversations by making explicit references to her daughter's nightmares while at the same time trying to get Graybo to admit that these nightmares were related to real events. Graybo's unfortunately (for him) ambiguous statement "*it* was a mistake" caused the police to indict him for molesting the child. He could have been more explicit, saying, "her dreams were a mistake." But he didn't identify his "it" and he was subsequently charged with sexual misconduct. In the same way his saying "I'm sorry for that" did not specify what he was sorry about, leaving this unclear because he was not explicit about his "that." The mother was no better in her referencing, saying things like "explain to her that you're not gonna do *what you did* to her again" and "why you *did it.*" One could argue, as the police may have, that since it is so difficult for a mother to utter the words "licked her vagina," it was only natural for her to avoid these painful words and instead use vague terms like "it" and "what you did." However true this may be, the only time the mother did manage to say "licked her vagina" Graybo vehemently denied it. The police monitoring her confrontation call apparently missed that Graybo had made no such agreements with her "it" and "what you did" offerings. These responses, according to Graybo's language, referred to his appearances in the girl's nightmares.

When Ken Martin's stepdaughter accused him of having sex with her, the most explicit ways she said this were "*the things* that we did" and "*what happened* in the past." The language evidence shows that Ken interpreted these ambiguous words to refer to the fights that he and his stepdaughter had in the past when he tried to tell her that *this* won't happen again. Regardless of the ambiguities, the police thought that Ken had agreed that he had sexually abused her. This was faulty intelligence analysis.

Even Stephen Ray (chapter 12) gave no language evidence of being consciously aware of the impact of his ambiguous use of "I know I *made a mistake.*" His language indicated that he believed his mistake was allowing his customer to fulfill her offer (even her reported desire, in fact) to give him oral sex. She had other accusations in mind, as did the police. If he had been less ambiguous about exactly what his mistake was, perhaps the prosecutor would have had a more difficult time charging him with sexual misconduct.

ANALYSIS OF GRAMMATICAL AND LEXICAL FEATURES

Finally, although grammatical and lexical features are often useful in the written language evidence of civil cases and in some criminal cases, these features did not play prominent roles in the eleven sexual misconduct cases discussed here. Unlike civil cases involving contracts or insurance policies, these participants gave no evidence of failing to understand the morphology, syntax, or word meanings.

In many ways, sexual misconduct cases are similar to other criminal law cases in which language is central to the analysis. Most of the same analytical tools are relevant and useful in the process of determining the significance of the evidence. In the case of sexual misconduct, however, identification and analysis of the speech event, the schemas, the speech acts, and the ambiguity of referencing proved to be most useful. As can be seen in the summary of their uses, the larger units of language consistently enlighten the smaller units. The logical conclusion, mentioned throughout the book, is to start the analysis with the large units and move down the inverted triangle step by step.

REFERENCES

Aubry, Arthur S., and Rudolph R. Caputo. 1980. *Criminal interrogation*. Springfield, IL: Charles C. Thomas.

Berk-Seligson, Susan. 2007. The elicitation of a confession: Admitting murder but resisting an accusation of attempted rape. In *The language of sexual crime*, ed. Janet Cotterill, 16–41. Basingstoke: Palgrave Macmillan.

Bok, Sissela. 1983. *Secrets*. New York: Vintage Books.

Black's Law Dictionary. 2004. ed. Bryan A. Garner. St.Paul MN: Thomson West.

Ceci, Stephen J., and Maggie Bruck. 1995. *Jeopardy in the courtroom: A scientific analysis of children's testimony*. Washington, DC: American Psychological Association.

Cotterill, Janet, ed. 2007. *The language of sexual crime*. Basingstoke, UK: Palgrave Macmillan.

Ehrlich, Susan. 2001. *Representing rape: Language and sexual consent*. London: Routledge.

Ehrlich, Susan. 2007. Normative discourses and representations of coerced sex. In *The language of sexual crime*, ed. Janet Cotterill. Basingstoke, UK: Palgrave Macmillan.

Feltz, Adam. 2008. The Knobe effect: A brief overview. *Journal of Mind and Behavior* 28: 265–277.

Godfrey, Drexel E., and Don R. Harris. 1971. *Basic elements of intelligence*. Washington, DC: U.S. Government Printing Office.

Gudjonsson, G.H. 1991.The application of interrogative suggestibility to police interviews. In *Human Suggestibility: Advances in Theory. ed. J.F.Schumaker, 51–82.*

Grice, H. P. 1975. Logic and conversation. 41–58 In *Syntax and semantics 3: Speech acts*, ed. Peter Cole and Jerry L. Morgan. New York: Academic Press.

Gudjonsson, Gisli. 1993. *The psychology of interrogations, confessions, and testimony*. New York: John Wiley.

Gumperz, John. 1990. *Language and social identity*. New York: Cambridge University Press.

Inbau, Fred, John E. Reid, and Joseph P. Buckley. 1986. *Criminal interrogation and confession*. Baltimore, MD: Williams and Wilkins.

Lakoff, Robin. 2000. *The language war*. Berkeley: University of California Press.

Leo, Richard. 2008. *Police interrogation and American justice*. Cambridge, MA: Harvard University Press.

Matoesian, Gregory M. 1993. *Reproducing rape: Domination through talk in the courtroom*. Chicago: University of Chicago Press.

Matoesian, Gregory M. 2001. *Law and the language of identity: Discourse in the William Kennedy Smith rape trial*. New York: Oxford University Press.

Mendoza-Denton, Norma. 1995. 121–141 Pregnant pause: Silence and authority in the Anita Hill–Clarence Thomas hearings. In *Gender articulated: Language and the culturally constructed self*, ed. Mary Bucholtz and Kira Hall. New York: Routledge.

Miller, George A. 1956. The magic number seven, plus two or minus two. *Psychological Review* 63(2): 81–97.

O'Hara, C.E & G.L O'Hara. 1988, *Fundamentals of Criminal Investigation*. Springfield IL: Charles C. Thomas.

Ong, Walter. 1982. *Orality and literacy: The technologizing of the word*. New York: Methuen.

Poole, Debra A., and Michael E. Lamb. 2002. *Investigative interviews with children*. Washington, DC: American Psychological Association.

Royal, Robert F. and Steven R. Schutt. 1976. *The gentle art of interviewing and interrogation: A professional manual and guide*. Upper Saddle River, NJ: Prentice Hall.

Searle, John R. 1969. *Speech acts*. Cambridge: Cambridge University Press.

Shuy, Roger W. 1982. Topic as the unit of analysis in a criminal law case. 113–126 In *Analyzing discourse: Text and talk*, ed. Deborah Tannen. Washington, DC: Georgetown University Press.

Shuy, Roger W. 1990. The analysis of tape recorded conversations. 117–148 In *Criminal intelligence analysis*, ed. Paul P. Andrews and Marylyn B. Peterson. Loomis, CA: Palmer Enterprises.

Shuy, Roger W. 1993. *Language crimes*. Oxford: Blackwell.

Shuy, Roger W. 1998. *The language of confession, interrogation and deception*. Thousand Oaks, CA: Sage.

Shuy, Roger W. 2001. Discourse analysis in the legal context. 437–452 In *The handbook of discourse analysis*, ed. Deborah Schiffrin, Deborah Tannen, and Heidi Hamilton. Oxford: Blackwell.

Shuy, Roger W. 2005. *Creating language crimes*. New York: Oxford University Press.

Shuy, Roger W. 2008. *Fighting over words*. New York: Oxford University Press.

Shuy, Roger W. 2011. *The language of perjury cases*. New York: Oxford University Press.

Solan, Lawrence. 2009. Blame, praise, and the structure of legal rules. *Brooklyn Law Review* 75(2): 517–543.

Solan, Lawrence M., and Peter M. Tiersma. 2005. *Speaking of crime*. Chicago: University of Chicago Press.

Staton, Jana, Roger W. Shuy, Joy Kreeft Peyton, and Leslee Reed. 1988. *Dialogue journal communication: Classroom, linguistic, social and cognitive views*. Norwood, NJ: Ablex.

Tannen, Deborah. 2007. *Talking voices*. New York: Cambridge University Press.

Tiersma, Peter. 1999. *Legal language*. Chicago: University of Chicago Press.

Tiersma, Peter. 2010. *Parchment paper pixels*. Chicago: University of Chicago Press.

Tiersma, Peter. 2007. The language of consent in rape law. In *The language of sexual crime*, ed. Janet Cotterill, 83–103. Basingstoke, UK: Palgrave Macmillan.

Walker, Anne G. 1990. Language at work in the law: The customs, conventions, and appellate court consequences of court reporting. 203–244 In *Language in the judicial process*, ed. Judith Levi and Anne G. Walker. New York: Plenum Press.

Wrightsman, Lawrence S., and Saul M. Kassin. 1993. *Confessions in the courtroom*. Newbury Park, CA: Sage.

Yeschke, C. L. 1987. *Interviewing: An introduction to interrogation*. Springfield, IL: Charles C. Thomas.

Cases cited

Bronston v. United States, 409 U.S. 352, 353 (1973)

Burlington Industries v. Kimberly Ellerth, 542 U.S. 742 (1998)

Harris v. Forklift Systems, Inc., 510 U.S. 17 (1993)

Farragher v. Boca Raton, 524 U.S. 775 (1998)

Kolstad v. American Dental Association, 527 U.S. 526 (1999)

Meritor Savings Bank v. Vincent, 477 U.S. 57 (1986)

People v. Evans, 85 Misc. 2d 1088, 379 N.Y.S. 2d 912 (1975)

INDEX